John N. Norton

Life of Bishop Wilson of Calcutta

John N. Norton

Life of Bishop Wilson of Calcutta

ISBN/EAN: 9783337849696

Printed in Europe, USA, Canada, Australia, Japan

Cover: Foto ©Lupo / pixelio.de

More available books at **www.hansebooks.com**

LIFE

OF

BISHOP WILSON,

OF

CALCUTTA.

BY THE

REV. JOHN N. NORTON, D.D.,

RECTOR OF ASCENSION CHURCH, FRANKFORT, KY.

AUTHOR OF "ROCKFORD PARISH;" "SHORT SERMONS;" "LIFE OF GENERAL WASHINGTON," ETC.

"He still lives by his good works, and has left, in his character and example, a rich inheritance to all time."—*Address of the Clergy of Ceylon.*

NEW YORK:

General Protestant Episcopal Sunday School Union and Church Book Society,

762 BROADWAY.

1863.

Entered, according to Act of Congress, in the year 1862,

By the GENERAL PROTESTANT EPISCOPAL SUNDAY SCHOOL UNION AND CHURCH BOOK SOCIETY,

In the Clerk's Office of the District Court of the United States for the Southern District of New York.

WILLIAM DENYSE,
STEREOTYPER AND ELECTROTYPER,
188 *William Street, N. Y.*

PUBLISHED

THROUGH THE

𝔒𝔣𝔣𝔢𝔯𝔦𝔫𝔤𝔰 𝔬𝔣 𝔱𝔥𝔢 𝔖𝔲𝔫𝔡𝔞𝔶 𝔖𝔠𝔥𝔬𝔬𝔩

OF

CHRIST CHURCH,

CAMBRIDGE,

MASSACHUSETTS.

TO

THE RT. REV. GREGORY T. BEDELL, D.D.,

Assistant Bishop of Ohio.

It was my privilege, during my Seminary course, to be a frequent attendant upon your ministrations in New York, and my first and only parish had received, in its early days, most generous assistance from yours, in remembrance of which it bears its name. These facts suggested the propriety of

Dedicating this Book to You.

I trust that the liberty thus taken may not be displeasing to you, since the memory of Bishop Wilson must be dear to your heart.

That God may grant you a long and honored career, like his, is the writer's humble prayer.

"BISHOP WILSON's energy, his truly evangelical love of souls, his distinguished liberality, his missionary spirit, his fearlessness in speaking out whatever he thought ought to be said, his simplicity and transparence of character, his love for Holy Scripture and for prayer, his fervent personal piety—all these rightly won for him the reverential affection of all who were brought near him."

Church Journal for April 4th, 1860.

"DANIEL WILSON was a model, as a Christian Bishop—the most admirable combination of evangelical truth and apostolic order of whom we have ever read. He dearly loved the Gospel. Christ was to him all in all. At eighty-six, he was as full of zeal and love for the salvation of souls as in the early hour of holy devotion to the ministry of reconciliation; and withal he was so sound, so true, so earnest a Churchman, in the very best sense of that much-abused word, that he seemed the imbodiment of the principles of our glorious Reformation, breathing the very spirit, as he held fast by the Scriptural doctrines, of the Prayer-Book."

Southern Episcopalian for May, 1860.

PREFACE.

As a college student, the writer used to recite, on Monday mornings, a very profitable lesson from Bishop Wilson's *Evidences of Christianity*—a work referred to in the narrative which follows. Having formed the acquaintance of this good man thus early in life, he always read with interest whatever was published, from time to time, concerning his abundant labors in India; and he regards it as a high privilege, indeed, that he is permitted, through these pages, to do something towards perpetuating his memory.

The life of Bishop Wilson, by his son-in-law and first chaplain, the Rev. Josiah Bateman, is a treasure-house of facts, and this unpretending volume could hardly have been prepared without it. But while the clergy will never complain of that work as being too long, there are thousands of the laity who would never find time to read it. We trust, therefore, that we are introducing the late Bishop of Calcutta to many who might otherwise have been almost strangers to him.

Whatever faults may be found in regard to arrangement or style, the writer is confident that all must give him credit for the strictest honesty of purpose, and a sincere desire to record nothing but the truth.

FRANKFORT, KY., *Nov.*, 1860.

From Greenland's icy mountains,
   From India's coral strand,
Where Afric's sunny fountains
   Roll down their golden sand;
From many an ancient river,
   From many a palmy plain,
They call us to deliver
   Their land from error's chain.

What though the spicy breezes
   Blow soft o'er Ceylon's isle,
Though every prospect pleases,
   And only man is vile:
In vain with lavish kindness
   The gifts of God are strewn;
The heathen in his blindness
   Bows down to wood and stone.

Shall we, whose souls are lighted
   With wisdom from on high—
Shall we to men benighted
   The lamp of life deny?
Salvation! oh, Salvation!
   The joyful sound proclaim,
Till each remotest nation
   Has learned Messiah's name!

                    BISHOP HEBER.

CONTENTS.

CHAPTER I.

Birth and parentage—Proper treatment for a puny infant—At school when seven years old—Placed under Mr. Hackney's care—"Not worth flogging"—Idleness cured—Engages in business—Some early reminiscences—Letter to a school companion—Routine of daily employment—A true portrait, with all its lights and shades—The heart under the degrading influences of sin—"Pray for the feelings"—God's gracious dealings—Finding peace for the soul........................... 15

CHAPTER II.

Difficulties in the way of entering the ministry—Consultations with several clergymen—His father consents to his leaving business—Enters St. Edmund's Hall—Mr. Pratt—Remembrances of the worthy Vice-President—Resistance of temptation—Confirmation—Letter to his mother—Passes the final examination with honor—Prize essay—Singular coincidence—Ordination—Becomes Mr. Cecil's curate—Abundant labors—Above the influence of petty jealousy—Appointed to a tutorship at Oxford—Marriage—Some account of Mr. Wilson's children 29

CHAPTER III.

Duties at Oxford—Curate of Worton—Attempts to benefit the undergraduates—Upper and Lower Worton—A striking contrast—"He knows almost everything"—Prosperity of Zion—Called to another field—St. John's, Bedford Row—Reason for making this change—Unselfishness—A scattered congregation soon rallied—The preaching of "Christ crucified"—Graphic picture—Interesting incidents—Large Confirmation—Evidences of pastoral fidelity—Outside labors—Scene at a dinner-table—Mrs. Fry—Habits of prayer—Failing health—Visit to the Continent—First lessons in the school of affliction 50

CHAPTER IV.

Mr. Wilson appears in another pulpit—Islington—The last incumbent—One party delighted, and the other apprehensive—The new Vicar's first sermon—Waiting the Lord's good time—Worldly wisdom—All difficulties harmonized—"No such thing as getting a comfortable game at cards!"—Sitting in the pulpit—Efforts for additional church accommodation—Difficulties in the way—The first meeting of the vestry—A third service begun—Improving health—Circular letter in regard to building new churches—The final adoption of the plan proposed—Application to the Church Commissioners—"I am like unto them that dream"—Fifteen Sunday-schools established.. 76

CHAPTER V.

A storm brewing—The afternoon lectureship—A long and painful struggle brought to a peaceable end—Persuasive influence—The Cross taken up—Severe affliction—Mrs. Wilson's sickness and death—"The same yesterday, and to-day, and forever"—Resignation—Large Confirmation—Preparation for first Communion—Prosperous condition of the parish—Consecration of the three new churches—Freedom from debt—Appointment of clergymen—The Lord's work prospering........ 91

CHAPTER VI.

The private journal once more resumed—Mr. Wilson enters upon his fifty-third year—Honest confessions of a contrite heart—Islington in an uproar—Cause of the disturbance—The prayer of faith receives an answer of peace—A voice from India—Death of Bishop Turner—Difficulty in finding a successor—Mr. Wilson offers to go—His motives scrutinized—Consecration—Preparations for leaving England—Sets sail for Calcutta 102

CHAPTER VII.

Making good use of a sea voyage—Daily routine on ship-board—Interesting letter to the Dean of Salisbury—The dark and bright sides of the picture—Desire to glorify God—An unexpected visitor—Ten days well spent—Affecting farewell—More diligent than before—Sickness breaks out—First sight of India—Landing at Calcutta 112

CHAPTER VIII.

The Bishop's installation—Kind address to the clergy—Jurisdiction of the Bishop of Calcutta in 1832—A wise division of so vast a field—First sermon in the Cathedral—General inspection of schools and missionary societies—The civilities of life—Bishop's Palace—"Enough for six months!"—Preparing to live—Marriage of a daughter—Two years for acclimation—Impossibility of pleasing everybody—Wisdom justified of her children—Personal habits—Modes of gaining information—Friendly and confidential intercourse with the Governor-General—Attending to business on horseback—"Lord William is less of a Churchman than I could desire".................... 120

CONTENTS. xi

CHAPTER IX.
PAGE

Details of labor—Difficulties in the Free School, and measures taken to reconcile them—Publication of Paine's "Age of Reason"—Lectures on the Evidences of Christianity—Clerical meetings—Their effects—Bishop's college—The new Bishop does his duty as a visitor—First Ordination in India—A holy week—Large Confirmation—The "seven duties"—Not too late—An awkward interruption—Conversion of the natives—The Bishop visits an interesting mission—Christianity and Paganism side by side—Baptism administered—"Good, good".. 129

CHAPTER X.

Unhappy divisions among Christians a hindrance to the Gospel—Bishop Wilson discourages a spirit of proselytism—Establishment of infant schools—Successful experiment—Extract from a Bengalee paper—The Bishop's efforts in behalf of steam navigation between England and India—The wide space bridged over by Oriental steamers—Renewal of the East India Company's charter—The King authorized to make some important changes in Church affairs—Bishop Wilson's joy at the dawn of better days—The Dioceses filled, and the new machinery set to work... 139

CHAPTER XI.

The want of suitable places for public worship—A feasible plan for remedying the evil—Its gratifying results—A knotty question, which led to some difficulties—The Bishop loses confidence in public men—Preparations for a visitation of his Diocese—His first charge to the clergy—Departure for Penang—What happened there—A flourishing nutmeg plantation, and its clerical owner—An amusing incident—Arrival at Singapore—Its religious destitution—Some important steps taken—Presbyterian scruples removed.. 150

CHAPTER XII.

Malacca caught napping—Result of the Bishop's visitation—Moulmein—Yellow robes and shaven heads—Hopeful prospects—Spicy breezes from Ceylon—Three weeks of constant labor—Dangerous passage to Madras—Narrow escape from shipwreck—An especial errand, and not a pleasant one—The caste question—No more half-way measures—Winnowing the chaff from the wheat—Time-serving policy of the Government—Proceeds to Tanjore—"The track of the holy and beloved Heber"—Reception at Tanjore—The old native priest—Secret aspirations... 160

CHAPTER XIII.

Most unpromising condition of affairs—Looking to God for help—Swartz's grave—Interesting services—Efforts to bring the native Christians to a better mind—Journey to Trichinopoly—Service in the Mission Church—Bishop Heber—The Caste question again—Meeting the difficulty boldly—Some changes for the better—Ordination at Tanjore—A rallying-point gained—Happy six months—Safe arrival at Calcutta.......... 176

CHAPTER XIV.

At home, but not idle—Changes in the Government, and departure of friends—An affecting duty—Lord William returns home—Perplexing questions settled—The Bishop resumes his visitation—Entrance gate to the Syrian churches—Brief account of them—Services at Quilon—Sets out for the interior—Preaches at Allepie—Attempts to benefit the Syrian Christians—The College at Cottayam—Bishop Wilson waited upon by the Syrian clergy—His conferences with them—"Never again shall I behold such a sight".......... 189

CHAPTER XV.

Hurrying onward to Cochin—Intercourse with white and black Jews—A word of exhortation, which was not very favourably received—Confirmation at Cochin—Visit to several Syrian churches—General impressions concerning their spiritual state—Old Goa—St. Francis Xavier—The City of Churches—Military station at Belgaum—Sixteen days spent in Bombay—Preparations for a long land journey.......... 199

CHAPTER XVI.

Poonah and Kirkee—New Year's blessing—Ready for marching—Horse and foot—The Sepoy guard—Order of proceedings—Temperance lecture—Enters the territories of the Nizam—A nice church, but one seldom used—The effects of plain preaching under certain circumstances—Lay reading recommended—The Bishop of Madras sends a warning, which is unheeded—Braving dangers Standing up for the order of the Church.. 211

CHAPTER XVII.

Jyepoor—Journey to Delhi—Mosques and palaces—Holy Week at Meerut—Four thousand Christians—A well-spent week—Confirmation—Visiting the sick—Sudden illness—Himalaya Mountains—Mussooree—Building a church—Deo gratias—Perilous journey—Arrival at Simlah—Four months' comparative rest—Preparing a volume of sermons for the press....... 222

CONTENTS.   xiii

CHAPTER XVIII.

PAGE

Again on the march—Transition from cool to hot—Takes boats at Roopur—No vain boast—The watch-house of Lahore—Journey to Kurnaul—First ordination of a Brahmin convert—Roman Catholic priests sent for in haste—Arrival at Delhi—Colonel Skinner's noble vow—Consecration of St. James' church—Impressive scene—Agra—Trying wheel-carriages—Condition of roads—New Year at Bareilly—Sowing in tears, and reaping in joy—Futtyghur—Cawnpore—Difficulties settled—Extensive charities—Futtchpore—Pilgrim tax—Abolition of an evil practice—Death of Bishop Corrie—Passage to Calcutta—Thanksgiving.. 235

CHAPTER XIX.

Home work once more—Funeral sermon for Bishop Corrie—A few weeks well filled up—Short missionary tour—City of Krishna—The faithful Weitbrecht—Scriptural names—An elephant teaching a lesson of patience—Loss of friends—The beginning of 1838—Prediction concerning the "Oxford School" of theology—Sermon by a Brahmin convert—Ignorance of decorum—Reflections on Easter Day—Entering upon his sixty-first year 250

CHAPTER XX.

Another charge to the clergy—"The Tracts for the Times"—Setting out on a second visitation—Remarkable answer to prayer—A new friend—Grief for the death of Sir Benjamin Malkin—State of Church affairs at Malacca—God's unsearchable judgments—Singapore—A whole community "coming round"—Chittagong—Sir William Jones—Arrival of a new chaplain—The Bishop resumes his old college duties—Course of Lent lectures—Plans for building a new cathedral—"My Lord, it is all yours"—Laying the corner-stone—The great work begun.. 261

CHAPTER XXI.

A Macedonian cry—Wonderful awakening among the natives—Putting the sickle into the harvest—The Bishop goes himself to share in the glorious work—Seventy-two native villages in one missionary circuit—The baptism at Anunda Bass—"We renounce them all"—The Bishop goes on his way rejoicing—A city set on a hill—Quiet rebuke, which accomplished its purpose—Land march begun—Two churches consecrated at Cawnpore—The same duty performed in other places—"Faint, yet pursuing"—A long journey safely ended.................. 273

CHAPTER XXII.

A few troubles to disturb the smooth current of events—Oxford theology again—The Plymouth Brethren make a convert—Efforts to bring back the wandering sheep—Watching the cathedral—All Calcutta mad after the world—A short visitation—Sunday at Sylhet—Riding in boats and on elephants—Chirra Poongee—Supremacy of the Holy Scriptures defended—First metropolitan visitation—Doings at Madras—Caste difficulties—Moving onward—Rhenia's tomb—Syrian churches—Disappointed hopes—At Bombay—Thanksgiving sermon on reaching home.. 281

CHAPTER XXIII.

On board ship—Works of faith and love—Serious illness—Consecration of church at Almorah—Preparing a book for his diocese—Farewell to Simlah—Another severe attack—The Bishop returns to Calcutta—Departure for England—Summary of thirteen years' labor—Once more at Islington—What was accomplished during his visit—A last farewell—Arrival at Calcutta—"I must go softly"—Consecration of the cathedral—"Dying charge"—A new visitation begun.................. 298

CHAPTER XXIV.

Reception at Bombay—Colombo—Over-work at Madras—Illness—Ordered to sea—New palace—Visitation resumed—Thirty-six days fully occupied—Consecration of a church in Borneo—Sickness of Professor Street—The differences between good men fading away—Growing old—Another faithful charge—Picture drawn by the Bishop of Victoria—Arrival of a grandson—Inauguration of the East India Railway—Consecration of the Bishop of Labuan.. 308

CHAPTER XXV.

Last charge to the clergy—Seventh visitation—Brave old man—Failing strength—His resolution to die at his post—The Indian mutiny—Trying the effect of sea air—Last Ordination—Confined to the bed—"I am talking in my sleep"—All is peace—Funeral solemnities—Brief epitome of his labors—Character—His benefactions—Peculiarities.. 319

LIFE OF
BISHOP WILSON.

Chapter First.

BIRTH AND PARENTAGE—PROPER TREATMENT FOR A PUNY INFANT—AT SCHOOL, WHEN SEVEN YEARS OLD—PLACED UNDER MR. HACKNEY'S CARE—"NOT WORTH FLOGGING"—IDLENESS CURED—ENGAGES IN BUSINESS—SOME EARLY REMINISCENCES—LETTER TO A SCHOOL COMPANION—ROUTINE OF EARLY EMPLOYMENT—A TRUE PORTRAIT, WITH ALL ITS LIGHTS AND SHADES—THE HEART UNDER THE DEGRADING INFLUENCES OF SIN—"PRAY FOR THE FEELINGS"—GOD'S GRACIOUS DEALINGS.

THE general interest felt in Bishop Heber by all Christian people, has brought India close to the hearts of thousands. Those who followed him in his high office might feel assured that there would be many to watch their labors and to rejoice in their success. But aside from any such adventitious circumstances, the subject of this memoir was quite too remarkable a man to make it necessary that his importance should be increased by borrowing from the reputation of others. Our readers cannot fail to be interested in tracing his eventful career.

Daniel Wilson, the eldest son of Stephen and Ann Collett (West) Wilson, was born in Church Street, Spitalfields, London, July 2d, 1778. His father was a silk manufacturer—a worthy and excellent man, and a devout Christian. Mrs. Wilson had early in life chosen "the good part," and was an exemplary wife and an affectionate mother.

Daniel, being a feeble infant, was sent to the country to be nursed, and to enjoy the benefits of purer air. By proper attention, he grew up to be a healthy, vigorous boy, and no one who observed his firm step, buoyant spirits, and intellectual countenance, would have supposed him to be the same person whose early days had been so unpromising.

At the age of seven, he was sent to a preparatory school at Eltham, in Kent. In his tenth year he was placed under the care of the Rev. John Eyre, in Hackney. This respected clergyman eked out the inadequate salary derived from the regular duties of his office by teaching a small school. He soon learned to appreciate the character of Daniel Wilson, and said: "There is no milk-and-water in the boy; he will be something, either very bad or very good."

One day, in a fit of idleness and perversity, the lad not only refused to do his accustomed work, but neglected an additional task which had been set him as a punishment. Mr. Eyre, passing through the room, saw he was wasting his time, and remarked, with some sharpness: "Daniel, you are not worth flogging, or I would flog you." This stirred the boy's pride at once, and he was never accused of idleness afterwards. Indeed, he became so persevering and pains-taking, that on one occasion, finding himself unable to master his appointed lesson, he declined going to breakfast, saying, "No; if my head will not work, my body shall not eat."

Mr. Eyre soon became proud of his pupil, and always spoke of him as possessing an intellect of the highest order. Daniel Wilson loved his teacher, and in after years he used to ask his advice in cases of doubt and difficulty. He remained at school until his fourteenth year, when he was taken into the warehouse of Mr. William Wilson, a near relative by blood, and his maternal uncle by marriage.

Daniel now found himself in a new world. His uncle was an extensive silk manufacturer and merchant—a strict and just man—expecting in others the industry and perseverance which he practised himself, and holding out the prospect of preferment to such as deserved it. Daniel thus speaks of this period of his life: "My parents, for the first years of their marriage, were a kind of loose Church people, from the want of piety in their parish ministers, attending regularly at Mr. Romaine's, of Blackfriars Church, in the morning of the Sunday, and at the Tabernacle, I suppose, in the evening. When their young family found the distance from Blackfriars inconvenient, they attended at a dissenting meeting-house in their neighborhood in the morning, and at Spitalfields Church in the evening. My schoolmaster, however, being a clergyman—though not strictly regular—I was accustomed to the Church service during the four years of my residence with him.

"When I went to live with my uncle, before I was fourteen, an entire change took place in these respects; for he was a strict and conscientious Churchman, attending first Mr. Romaine, and after his death, Mr. Crowther, of Christ Church, Newgate Street, Mr. Cecil, Mr. Scott, and Mr. Basil Woodd. My prejudices, therefore (for I had no religion), were then in favor of the Church of England, and though the predilection was slight before I went to college, it became, from the moment I entered the University, so deeply conscientious, that I have never done any one act inconsistent with the bonds of that communion from that period."

The records of his first three years of service are somewhat scanty. His daily duties are described in the following letter to a school companion (named Vardy), with whom, for a short time, he carried on an active correspondence.

"*February* 16, 1797.

"My individual employment is not laborious, but it is constant. Our usual hours of work are from six o'clock in the morning till eight o'clock in the evening, in the summer; and from seven o'clock in the morning till eight in the evening, in winter, so that you see I have but little time to myself. After eight o'clock, in general, I am at liberty to read or write alone, till supper-time, which is at half-past eight o'clock or a quarter of nine; and after this I sit reading with the family till ten o'clock, when my uncle calls them to prayers, and all go to bed. But as my leisure moments were by these regulations exceedingly circumscribed, I have always been accustomed to spend a couple of hours in my room before I retired to rest.

Then I used constantly to study my Latin and French, so that I am making considerable progress in both."

As it is our purpose to give a true portrait of Daniel Wilson, unbiassed by prejudice, we must allow him to mention some things in regard to his early religious character, not much to his credit. We can not, however, fail to admire the straightforward honesty which led him to acknowledge his faults.

"As far back as I can remember [he says] my whole heart was given to sin. Even when a boy at school, when particular circumstances recur to my mind, I am shocked at the dreadful depravity of my nature as it then discovered itself. I have indeed proceeded in a regular progression from the less sins of bad books, bad words, and bad desires, to the grosser atrocities of those emphatically known as 'the lusts of the flesh.' I was constantly acting against a better knowledge. I had received a religious education, and had been accustomed to a regular attendance on public ordinances. I could criticise a sermon, and talk and dispute about particular notions; but I loved my sins, and could not bear to part with them. I never had gone so far as to deny any one of the doctrines of the Gospel. I acknowledged them to be true, but for want of that necessary attendant, self-application, I could hear whole sermons, but not a word belonged to me! I took a false idea of the Gospel, and, from this distorted view, dogmatically pronounced it out of my power to do anything; and so, hushing my conscience with 'having done all I could,' I remained very quietly the willing slave of sin and Satan."

The atmosphere of the warehouse in which Daniel Wilson passed his time was by no means favorable for growth in grace, or even for much serious thought. All was bustle and confusion during the day, and at night, when the restraint of the master's presence was withdrawn, the young men indulged in much vain discourse, and I am sorry to add that our holy religion was spoken of with little reverence or respect. The spirit of the age was skeptical, and it is hardly to be wondered at that a youth full of self-will, and fond of self-indulgence, should yield to surrounding temptations, and be found at last sitting with composure in the seat of the scorner.

But the HOLY SPIRIT did not cease to strive with him, and he thus describes some of God's gracious dealings with him: "One evening (March 9th, 1796), I was, as usual, engaged in wicked discourse with the other servants in the warehouse, and religion happening (humanly speaking, I mean) to be started, I was engaged very warmly in denying the responsibility of mankind, on the supposition of absolute election, and the folly of all human exertions where grace was held to be irresistible. (I can scarcely proceed for wonder that God should have upheld me in life at the moment I was cavilling and blaspheming at His sovereignty and grace.) We have a young man in the warehouse whose amusement for many years has been entirely in conversing on the subject of religion. He was saying that God had appointed the end—he had also appointed the means. I then happened to say that I had none of those feelings towards God which he required and approved. 'Well, then,' said he, 'pray for the feelings.' I carried it off with a joke, but the words at the first made some impression on my mind, and thinking that I would still say 'I had done all I could,' when I retired at night I began to pray for the feelings. It was not long before the Lord in some measure answered my prayers, and I grew very uneasy about my state."

Young Wilson immediately sought an interview with his old teacher, Mr. Eyre, and the letters which passed between them showed how earnest the penitent must have been in his inquiries after truth, and how faithful the spiritual adviser whose counsels had been asked. His parents were soon made acquainted with his state of mind, and in reply to a letter from his anxious mother, he writes as follows:

April 7, 1796.

"I have received your letter, and would answer in sincerity your solemn query, How is it between God and your soul?

"What shall I say? How is it between the great omnipotent God, the creator and preserver of my life, in whom I live and move and have my being, and the soul of me, a worm of the earth, who exists only at His will? Awful thought! But this is not all. How is it between a just and holy God —a God of infinite purity—and my soul full of corruption and pride? How can I answer such a query?

"But when I add to these considerations, that while this God has been blessing me with the blessings of His providence, while He has been continuing me in life, and preserving me from every danger, I have been transgressing against Him in the most aggravated manner, against light and knowledge, and even now daily transgress against Him; I say, when I think on this question in connection with these ideas, I know not what to reply.

"This I know and feel, that I have forfeited His favor; that in me does not my help lie; that the curse of God is upon me, and that it is because He is God, and not man, that it has not long ago been executed. This also I am sensible of, that the curse may be executed this night, that my breath is in my nostrils, and that if I this night should be cut off, I should sink—where? Into that tremendous place where the 'worm dieth not, and the fire is not quenched.'

"But I have cried unto the Lord for mercy, and do endeavor still to cry unto Him, from, as it were, the very mouth of hell. And I have some faint hopes that the Lord will be merciful unto me and bless me. And this pursuit I hope and trust I shall never relinquish till I am blessed with an answer of peace.

"Oh! my dear mamma, it is not the pleasures of this life, nor the possession of its vain riches or honors which I seek after. No; but it is even the happiness of my immortal soul, which must exist for ever and ever. Oh! may the word ETERNITY never enter my ears without impressing my heart."

At the time of which we are speaking, that excellent man, the Rev. John Newton, was rector of St. Mary Woolnoth, and Daniel Wilson, who had often attended upon his ministry, now derived much benefit from his counsels and prayers. For months and months, however, he continued to have doubts and misgivings, and to distrust his own purposes of good; but at last he was enabled to throw himself unreservedly upon the promises of God in Christ Jesus. On the first Sunday in October, 1797, he received the Lord's Supper at the hands of Mr. Eyre, drawing near in faith, and taking " that holy Sacrament to his comfort." In speaking of this important step, in a letter to a young friend, he remarks: "Never did I enjoy so much the presence of my dear Redeemer, as I have since that time; and this, not so much in great sensations of pleasure, as in brokenness of heart, and, I trust, in sincere desires to be devoted to His glory. *Yesterday and to-day have been, I think, the happiest days I ever remember.* The Lord shines so upon my soul, that I can not but love *Him*, and desire no longer to live to myself, but to Him. And to you I confess it (though it ought, perhaps, to be a cause for shame), that I have felt great desires to go or do anything to spread the name of Jesus, and that I have even wished, if it were the Lord's will, to go as a missionary to heathen lands."

Chapter Second.

DIFFICULTIES IN THE WAY OF ENTERING THE MINISTRY—CONSULTATIONS WITH SEVERAL CLERGYMEN—HIS FATHER CONSENTS TO HIS LEAVING BUSINESS—ENTERS ST. EDMUND'S HALL—MR. PRATT—REMEMBRANCES OF THE WORTHY VICE-PRINCIPAL—RESISTANCE OF TEMPTATION—CONFIRMATION—LETTER TO HIS MOTHER—PASSES THE FINAL EXAMINATIONS WITH HONOR—PRIZE ESSAY—SINGULAR COINCIDENCE—ORDINATION—BECOMES MR. CECIL'S CURATE—ABUNDANT LABORS—ABOVE THE INFLUENCE OF PETTY JEALOUSY—APPOINTED TO A TUTORSHIP AT OXFORD—MARRIAGE—SOME ACCOUNT OF MR. WILSON'S CHILDREN.

ALTHOUGH Daniel Wilson's thoughts were now turned towards the sacred ministry, and friends with whom he advised encouraged him to prosecute his studies, there were difficulties in the way not easy to be overcome. His father was decidedly opposed to this plan, having entertained sanguine hopes that his son might become a successful man of business; and he had occasional apprehensions himself that his desire to become a clergyman might be only another evidence of the pride of heart which was one of his besetting sins.

Mr. Eyre and Mr. Newton were consulted, and, after some time of anxious suspense, the idea occurred to him that the Rev. Rowland Hill might help him to discover the path of duty. The young man was kindly received by the eccentric clergyman of Surrey Chapel, who inquired minutely into his family relations, his motives, and wishes, and finally expressed a hope that if the thing was really of the Lord, it might eventually prosper. This interview with Mr. Hill was followed, some months afterwards, by one with the Rev. Richard Cecil (one of the excellent of the earth); and at last all obstacles were happily removed, and with a heart full of thankfulness he makes this record in his private journal:

"Oh! the wonders of the Lord's goodness! My dear father let me go to Mr. Cecil's and Mr. Goode's, and they, after due examination, gave their opinion that I was called of

God to the ministry. *My father consented to my leaving business.* In a few days I am to go and enter myself at St. Edmund's Hall. Oxford, and be at Mr. Pratt's as a private pupil till I am ready to reside in college. My dear uncle has conducted himself with the greatest kindness during the whole matter, and has readily consented to the arrangement made by my father. The Lord has led me by a way that I knew not. To His great name be all the glory!"

In accordance with the plan thus proposed, Daniel Wilson went up to Oxford, and entered himself at St. Edmund's Hall, on the 1st of May; and in the same month he writes to his mother from Doughty Street, Russell Square, where the Rev. Josiah Pratt then resided:

"The desire you expressed to hear from me as soon as I was comfortably settled here has not been forgotten. I am encircled with mercies. In every point of view I find myself, as to outward circumstances, in the best possible situation. Mr. and Mrs. Pratt are extremely good-tempered and agreeable, and very pious. My fellow-students (two), though not serious, have been educated in a Moravian college, and are very civil, moral youths. I have a most beautiful prospect from my room over the fields, unobstructed by any houses. So much as to outward blessings; but these are nothing compared with spiritual, though all should excite gratitude from him who is unworthy of any."

At the age of twenty, Daniel Wilson began in good earnest to prepare himself for that holy calling which he was so long to adorn by his life and conversation. He not only applied himself with all diligence to study, but improved every favorable opportunity of doing good to his former companions, who might have received injury from his evil example in time past. The vice-principal of St. Edmund's Hall, at this period, was the Rev. Isaac Crouch, who exercised a most beneficial influence over the young men intrusted to his care. Thirty-four years afterwards, Daniel Wilson, writing to him from the Indian Ocean, says: "I look back now with fond delight to my introduction to you on April 30th, 1798. I recall your friendly advice, cautions, and instructions. I remember the Greek Testament lectures (of which I have my short-hand notes still), the delightful dinner parties, the Sunday-evening readings, the various scenes where I used to see your friendly countenance, and where I used to pass such happy hours with Mr. Greig, William Marsh, Cawood, and others. Many and many a reflection, dropped by you in conversation, now returns to my mind with double force. Accept, then, once more, my best acknowledgments. I have now in my cabin your present of Van-der-Hooght's Hebrew Bible, given me by you in 1801. It has been my companion ever since. Its binding has become again as old as that which you replaced by so splendid an exterior, thirty-two years back."

Our young collegian was thrown amongst those, at Oxford, who were extravagant in their habits, and who ran recklessly into debt; but he so carefully husbanded the hundred guineas a year which his father allowed him, that his expenses were kept within his income, although a desire to possess some new or valuable book was a temptation hard to be resisted.

The Church very properly permits persons to come to the Holy Communion before they have received the apostolic rite of "laying on of hands," in case they are "ready and desirous to be confirmed." It was on this condition that Daniel Wilson had been admitted to the Lord's Supper. On the 7th of June, 1799, he was confirmed by the Bishop of Chester, the Bishop of Oxford (Dr. Smallwell) being then too ill to discharge the duties of his office. Months passed away with little worthy of record. After spending the holidays in the bosom of his father's family, we find him once more at the University, entering upon his third and last year. A letter to his mother, dated January 12th, 1801, discloses the state of his mind and heart.

"The time I spent with you in town appears to me now like a dream that is passed away. Thus it is that our life is hastening along. One scene presents itself, and then vanishes; a second follows, and disappears in like manner. Now we are well; anon sickness seizes us. At this moment, everything is prosperous and comfortable; the next, all is dark and miserable.

"From reflecting upon these changes, however, we may learn two important lessons—the one solemn, the other encouraging. It is a solemn consideration that, amidst all the fluctuations of life, we are still making rapid advances towards eternity. Every wave, whether placid or turbulent, wafts us nearer to that awful shore. Like a ship which continues to make its way, whatever the passengers on board may be doing, we are perpetually hurried forward, whatever may be our employments.

"But as this is a solemn thought, so is it encouraging to contrast the uncertainty of all things here below with the unchangeableness of our gracious and Almighty Lord. This is our safety, that there is *One* who hath said, 'Because I live, ye shall live also;' and that there is an unfailing fountain of love and mercy in Him to remedy all the evils of time, and to crown us with every blessing.

"The more Satan can bring us to look upon the waves, the sooner we shall sink. It is when faith is fastened upon a crucified Jesus, that peace dwells in the heart, and holiness adorns the life and conversation. God gives us this 'precious faith,' that, looking unto the great Captain of our salvation, and receiving every supply from his fulness, we may go on our way rejoicing. The command is, 'Rejoice in the Lord always.' May the Lord the Spirit produce in us continually, and enable us to know more of the power of that kingdom which is righteousness and peace and joy in the Holy Ghost."

Young Wilson had applied himself so closely to study during his whole college course, that the approach of the final examination—an occasion of so much alarm to the dissipated and idle—gave him no particular uneasiness. He passed the trying ordeal with great credit to himself, and carried off the prize for an English essay on COMMON SENSE. It is an interesting fact, that when he descended the rostrum, amidst the applause of the audience, REGINALD HEBER arose to recite his poem of "Palestine."

There is something affecting in the picture of these two young aspirants, thus brought together in the morning of life, who were afterwards called to bear "the heat and burden of the day" in the same far distant field; something, also, in the scrolls they held, characteristic of the men—the one, throwing over India the charm of poetry, piety, and a loving spirit; the other, stamping upon it the impress of Scriptural supremacy and evangelical truth; something of adaptation, also, in the divine ordering of those consecrated spots where "they rest in their graves" —the chancel of *St. John's*, Trichinopoly, and the chancel of *St. Paul's*, Calcutta.

Daniel Wilson himself referred in after life to this meeting in the Oxford Theatre:

"Is it not a singular coincidence," he said, "that Heber, my revered, able, and pious predecessor, delivered his poem of 'Palestine' on the very day that I delivered my English prose essay on 'Common Sense?' I well remember, as I came down from the rostrum, seeing Heber, who sat immediately behind, testifying his applause in the kindest manner, though I never made his acquaintance till July 26th, 1812, when Mr. Thornton introduced him to me at St. John's Chapel, Bedford Row, after hearing me preach from Hebrews ii. 3.*

Mr. Wilson began his ministry under very favorable auspices—as curate, or assistant, of the Rev. Mr. Cecil, rector of Cobham, a pleasant agricultural village in Surrey, and Bisley, a retired hamlet three miles distant. He makes the following entry in his journal, in regard to this most important step:

"I am now numbered amongst the dressers

---

* Bateman's Life of Wilson, p. 51.

Bp. Wilson. Chobham Church in 1801. p. 38.

of God's vineyard. I entered into holy orders on the 20th September, by the imposition of hands of the Bishop of Winchester. Whilst Mr. Cecil is absent, I shall have two sermons to preach weekly—one at Cobham, and one at Bisley. All difficulties having been removed by the help of God, I am now happily discharging my sacred functions. What I had prepared, being committed to memory, I was enabled to deliver freely. Nor have I to complain of any unkind reception; on the contrary, I have to acknowledge, with gratitude to God, that it was far beyond my expectations.

"In my first sermon, I treated of the willingness of Christ to receive sinners coming unto him. 'Him that cometh unto me I will in no wise cast out.' In the second, I endeavored to explain the peace which Christ gave to His disciples—'Peace I leave with you.' Grant, Almighty God, that these things, which by Thy grace have happily begun, may by Thy power be brought to a good result."

Towards the close of the year, the young clergyman was left with the whole duty of the parish upon him, which called forth all his energies, and taxed his strength to the utmost.

Besides preaching three times a week, he was most faithful in visiting his people—going into every mud hut, and obtaining from Mr. Cecil himself (a man not accustomed to deal in empty compliments) the name of "The Apostle Wilson."

He began at first by writing his sermons fully out, and committing them to memory; but he soon adopted the plan of taking up notes only into the pulpit.

His journal furnishes many little incidents which serve to illustrate his character.

"I clearly perceive that my preaching is very bad," he remarks in one place. "It is all 'vi et armis.' I make clamor and shouting and noise my helpers—as if sound without sense ever did any good. I must spare no pains to correct these faults, now I know them. I only grieve most deeply, that when

Mr. Cecil in the kindest manner mentioned them to me, I perceived a secret sensation of anger, when I ought to have felt nothing but gratitude."

Some persons are so mean-spirited as to feel jealous whenever another is commended for qualities which they are sensible of possessing themselves in a smaller degree. Not so with Mr. Wilson. On one occasion, when he went up to Oxford for a short time, his place was supplied by his friend Marsh. We find this record in his journal, upon his return:

"Praises of all kinds were showered on him, my people were so struck with his countenance, his address, his sermons, his courtesy, that they lauded him to the skies— God be praised!"

Having labored two years at Cobham, some things occurred which changed his plans for the future. The following is his own account of the first of these events:

"January 23, 1803. I have wonderful things to record. I have refused the curacy of Henley, which has been offered to me, because, when I came here, I engaged to stay with Mr. Cecil three years. This being settled, lo! another matter, much more serious, occurs. Mr. Crouch wishes to know whether I should be willing to return to Oxford, and, conjointly with himself, undertake the office of tutor at St. Edmund's Hall. It is to be with this understanding, that the lighter part of the duty falls upon me at first, but that I should be prepared eventually to take the whole burden. The question is under consideration. The Principal has to be sounded. Mr. Cecil must be consulted and persuaded. Almost everything wants arrangement. May God's will be done! This alone grieves and vexes me, that, with so great a matter hanging over me, I am so feeble in mind, so full of sin, so backward in prayer, watchfulness, and submission."

The same subject is again referred to on the 9th of March, a day never forgotten by him:

"Seven years have passed since the grace

of God came with power to me, who was buried in total darkness. I acknowledge myself to be the vilest of the vile, and I grieve over it. Still the grace of God is exceedingly abundant towards me. I wish to be nothing, and would cleave to Christ only.

"The Oxford business is approaching its completion. The Principal has consented. My parents acquiesce. Mr. Cecil, though disinclined, does not absolutely refuse. I have written to Mr. Crouch to say that I shall be ready to undertake it as soon as I have fulfilled my engagement to remain with Mr. Cecil for three years. This must be done, unless Mr. Crouch can find some one whom Mr. Cecil would be willing to take in my place, and thus set me free. The will of the Lord be done."

Several months passed away before Mr. Wilson could secure a successor for his curacy, and it was not until November that he preached his farewell sermon and took his leave. Large congregations assembled to hear his parting counsels, and many tears were shed.

The other event to which we referred was the marriage of the young clergyman with his cousin Ann, the daughter of his uncle, Mr. William Wilson, to whom he had been tenderly attached for several years. The ceremony took place on the 23d of November, 1803.

A few words in regard to family matters, in this place, will not be amiss, especially as the happiness of Mr. Wilson for many years afterwards was greatly increased by his union with this lovely and excellent woman. As a daughter, she had her father's testimony that she had never given him one hour's uneasiness; and after the death of a beloved mother, she had been a guide and protector to her younger sisters. Although naturally inclined to silence and reserve, when she became a clergyman's wife she gave up her habits of retirement, and interesting herself in her husband's work, she presided over his household with dignity and grace, and discharged her appropriate duties in the fear of God.

In November, 1805, his eldest son, Daniel, was born; in September, 1807, his second son, John; in June, 1809, his daughter, Amelia. These three were born in Oxford.

In November, 1811, a second daughter, Ann Margaret, was born; in March, 1814, a third daughter, Eliza Emma; and in November, 1816, a third son, William. These were born in London. Thus God "made him an house," and for nearly fourteen years (with one sad interruption, occasioned by the death of his infant daughter, Amelia, in 1809) the voice of joy and health was heard in it.

Mr. Wilson was always too much occupied with the duties of his office to spend much time with his children, and while he was ready to promote their good at any sacrifice, he did not enter into their pursuits, and was not as patient with them as some are. At the same time, probably no parent ever suffered more acutely than he did when they were sick or in trouble.

After the death of little Ann, in 1818, he thus pours out his heart, in a letter to Mrs. Hannah More: "It is impossible for me to describe to you what we are going through. After the sudden death of one child—a lovely girl, about six years and a half old—a second child has been seized with sickness, and has now continued for above seven weeks in a most affecting and alarming state. We are watching our dear little boy dying before our eyes. He has been for eight days in perpetual convulsions, except as opiates compose for a time his agitated frame. The afflicted mother hangs over her suffering child with an anguish I cannot describe. Thus it pleases our heavenly Father to exercise us with by far the most severe trial we have ever known.

"For myself, as a minister of the sanctuary, I am quite assured that God 'in very faithfulness has caused me to be troubled.' I want bringing down. The natural tendency of my mind is towards excessive activity and bustle, with all the secret love of display and the praise of men which accompanies such a turn of character. I have now gone on seventeen years in the sacred ministry, with a large share of health and spirits, with some success in the great work of 'reconciliation' intrusted to me. Some late circumstances, in which I had, however, very little personal effort, have brought me still more before the public eye, and now my heavenly Father chastens me for my profit, that I may be a partaker of His holiness. He takes me aside from my public duties to private self-examination, and he calls me from preaching to praying—from the instruction of others to the instruction of myself. He bids me look inward, and take the guage and measure of my heart. He commands me to be silent, and contrite, and interior in my religion. He is preparing me for comforting, perhaps, the minds of others with the comfort wherewith I myself am comforted of God; and whilst he confines me to the chamber of sorrow, is perhaps fitting me in some better manner to discharge those high and elevated duties of a steward of the mysteries of God which I have so little honored as I ought. Oh, that I may learn softness, confession, humility, and tenderness in this school of suffering!"

The little boy spoken of in this letter recovered partially from this dangerous attack, and having survived until five years old, an object of solicitude and tender sympathy, he gently passed away.

Mr. Wilson's eldest-born, Daniel, was a great comfort to his parents, and became a useful clergyman—still being spared to labor for the good of souls.

John, the second son, was led away from the path of duty by the seductions of bad companions, and finally retired to the Continent, where he died in August, 1833, sincerely penitent for his faults, and at peace with God and man. His father was then in India, but his brother ministered at his dying couch. He was patient under the most intense sufferings, and thankful for every mercy, receiving the Holy Sacrament humbly, and finding it a means of grace to his soul.

We have preferred to bring together these items concerning family matters, that the regular course of the narrative may not be interrupted by them hereafter.

Chapter Third.

DUTIES AT OXFORD—CURATE OF WORTON—ATTEMPTS TO BENEFIT THE UNDER-GRADUATES—UPPER AND LOWER WORTON—A STRIKING CONTRAST—"HE KNOWS ALMOST EVERY THING!"—CALLED TO ANOTHER FIELD—ST. JOHN'S, BEDFORD ROW—REASON FOR MAKING THIS CHANGE—UNSELFISHNESS—A SCATTERED CONGREGATION SOON RALLIED—THE PREACHING OF "CHRIST CRUCIFIED"—GRAPHIC PICTURE—INTERESTING INCIDENTS—LARGE CONFIRMATION—EVIDENCES OF PASTORAL FIDELITY—OUTSIDE LABORS—SCENE AT A DINNER-TABLE—MRS. FRY—HABITS OF PRAYER—FAILING HEALTH—VISIT TO THE CONTINENT—FRESH LESSONS IN THE SCHOOL OF AFFLICTION.

N the year 1804, Mr. Wilson was residing with his family in Oxford, where his collegiate office occupied him during the week, his Sundays being employed in officiating as curate of Worton. When he began his duties at St. Edmund's Hall, he held a subordinate position, having Mr. Crouch to lean upon for counsel, and to aid him in difficulties. Three years afterwards, when his old friend retired from office, his responsibili-

ties were greatly increased. He thus writes, in January, 1807:

"Our friend Mr. Crouch has now resigned to me the whole management of the Hall; and utterly incompetent, I am left alone. I can scarcely tell what I am to do, and what leave undone. Nevertheless, I must follow the leadings of God's providence.

"The number of young men in the Hall at present, and the measure of their attainments, are not, perhaps, beyond my reach; but what plans may be adopted for the future I know not. You will easily understand how much I am engaged, when I tell you that this next term I have to lecture on Aristotle and the tragedies of Æschylus; that the New Testament has to be critically and copiously dealt with, and Aldrich's 'Ars logica' to be entered on. I will do what I can. If I cannot do for my pupils all that my wishes and the duties of my office require, yet nothing shall be wanting that good-will, kindness, and careful study can accomplish.

"It seems to me that my main object must

be so to instruct them in the saving knowledge of God, and so to imbue their minds (as much as in me lies) with true piety, that however little they may profit by me in secular matters, they may nevertheless learn to love God, to believe in Christ, and reject the vain traditions and fancies of men, to estimate aright the value of the soul, and to know and be ready to proclaim the excellent glory of the Cross. If they know and understand these things savingly and experimentally, they know all.

"So far as all this goes, my opinions remain unchanged and immoveable, though I know well that I am unable to follow them diligently, or carry them out successfully by my own power and might."

Besides the regular lectures and other instructions, Mr. Wilson sought to be useful to the under-graduates, by inviting them, in small parties, to the familiar intercourse of his house and table. His good intentions were, however, in a measure, defeated by a gravity and coldness of manner which left an unpleasant impression, making even social gatherings partake too much of the character of meetings for business and duty. His pupils, however, honored and admired him, and his influence was very generally felt. Thus much for his college duties.

His pastoral labors at Worton are those in which we feel most interest. There are two Wortons—Upper and Lower—little villages lying between Bambury and Woodstock, in Oxfordshire; the population consisting of farmers and agricultural laborers, and both places united not exceeding two hundred souls. A small church belonged to each village, where the people enjoy the privileges of religious worship.

Some of Mr. Wilson's predecessors in this curacy had been extremely careless in the performance of their duties, and every thing had fallen into sad neglect.

The contrast between this and his earnest and laborious ministry must have been very striking. At the close of the year 1803, he thus writes to his mother:

"I am called a laborer, a minister, an ambassador, a worker with God; may I fulfil the solemn duties which these titles imply, and which they require of me! An idle laborer, a careless minister, an unfaithful steward, a false ambassador, a sleeping watchman, will bring down upon himself a tenfold destruction.

"I wish, my dear mother, to be more like Mary sitting at the feet of Jesus, and learning His words. I wish to be more like Isaiah, who cried aloud and spared not, in showing his people their transgressions, and the house of Israel their sins; I wish to be more like St. Paul, instant in season and out of season, reproving, rebuking, exhorting, with all long-suffering and doctrine; above all, it is my prayer to have in me the same mind which was also in Christ Jesus, to have Christ formed in me, to walk worthy of the Lord unto all well-pleasing, being fruitful in every good work, and abounding in the knowledge of God.

"I have now two parishes on my hands,

where death and sin and darkness have reigned uncontrolled. Jesus is here unknown, grace is here a stranger, holiness is neither understood nor desired. All is under the power of the 'strong man armed.' But the Bible teaches me a charm which has a sovereign efficacy: 'I, if I be LIFTED UP, will draw all men unto me.' 'The weapons of our warfare are not carnal, but *mighty through God*.' 'We have this treasure in earthen vessels, that the *excellency of the power* may be of God, and not of us.' These are my first principles. This is my system. I desire to preach 'peace by Jesus Christ,' and then pray for the spirit of Jesus to apply it savingly to the heart and conscience. I am only ashamed that I do it so weakly and imperfectly."

Throwing aside all stiffness and formality, the zealous curate endeavored to adapt himself to the capacities of his rustic congregations, and illustrations for his discourses were freely drawn from the seed, the sack, the common, or the farmer, husbandman, and gardener. On one occasion he had been preaching on the resurrection of the body, and had dwelt upon the dying of the grain of wheat ere it springs up to new life. Two farmers were standing by the porch, after service, when one remarked: "There, you see, he knows a'most every thing. He told us truly how the seed dies afore it grows. He is not like our parson, who scarcely knows the difference between a cow and the moon."

"I remember," said a laboring man, who had been referred to for recollections of these days, "when one time he was speaking of victory over sins of the heart, and he impressed his thoughts upon us by saying, in his earnest way, 'Now, if you want to subdue sin in your hearts, you must encourage all that is holy there. He who will keep tares out of the sack, must fill it up with wheat.'"

Doddington is a large village in the immediate neighborhood, and the people were busy enclosing the common. "Mark," he said, "the way to heaven is not like an open common, with very many ways running through it, but a road fenced on both sides by the word of God."

Occasionally, there was a rapidity of utterance in the pulpit, and an impetuosity of manner; but this was not habitual or constant. His delivery was quiet and deliberate, and so distinct that the whole sermon was often taken down, in common writing, from his lips. He was very close in his appeals to conscience, and so solemn and impressive in his warnings and exhortations, as to produce a trembling awe. "Pray, do not let Mr. Wilson preach here again," said a lady to her minister, in an adjoining parish, "he alarms me so!" And this was doubtless sometimes true, for he was in earnest, and could almost say, with the Apostle, "Whether we be beside ourselves, it is to God; and whether we be sober, it is for your cause; for the love of Christ constraineth us."

The effect of all this was not sudden, but progressive, and it may encourage some who think that they are laboring in vain, and spending their strength for nought, to listen to his own account. In July, 1804, he writes to his friend Mr. Pearson: "My Worton flock improves very little, if you speak of true religion. I cannot, however, say that my ministry has been altogether unsuccessful." In May, 1806, he writes again: "We are going on well in our churches. The congregations are numerous and attentive; and on Sunday last we had fifty-eight communicants. I hope the Lord is doing something for us, and that several are seeking a better country, even a heavenly."

Again, in January, 1807: "A certain measure of success attends me at Worton. The congregations are numerous for the place. They hear and receive gladly the divine Word, but very few attain to salvation. Pour upon us, O Holy Spirit! thy heavenly grace, that the dead may hear Thy voice and live."

During the long vacation of the same year, he says: "Affairs prosper now at Worton.

We have a Wednesday service as well as on Sundays. The church is crowded. It is delightful to see such a great company listening to the word of God; whilst we may hope that many will be endued with divine life, and attain to heavenly blessedness."

Great good was accomplished through all the country about Worton, and the little churches were not only crowded, but many stood in the churchyard during the whole of the service and sermon, and large numbers of communicants came to the altar of the Lord.

A marble tablet over the entrance of Upper Worton church stands as a memorial of the faithful curate who there once dispensed the bread of life.

In the year 1809, Mr. Wilson was called to a more important field of labor. He thus writes from Oxford to his friend Pearson: "At Christmas last, Mr. Cecil sent for me to Clifton, and urged me to take St. John's as his curate, when my assistant at St. Edmund's Hall should be in a situation to act alone. I objected strongly on the ground of St. John's not being suitable to my cast of character; but this difficulty being removed by the assurance he gave me of the universal approbation manifested when I have taken duty for him, I then agreed that, in the course of two or three years, if God should please, I would yield to his wishes. With these impressions I left Clifton, and scarcely thought further of the affair, till a letter from him reached me about a month back, to state that his health was very rapidly declining, that things were falling to pieces at the chapel, and to urge me to take it wholly, as minister, whilst his life remained to him and the power to consign it legally.

"I was seized with the utmost consternation, and the moment the term closed, hurried to London to weigh the summons. I found Mr. Cecil too far gone to be capable of giving advice, but his mind was fixed on me as his successor. I stated to Mr. Cardale and the principal people of the chapel, all my difficulties, arising from Mr. Hill, my proposed successor at the Hall, being yet an under-graduate, and incapable of being left. No obstacle would divert them from their entreaties, and I yielded at length, on the supposition that no impediment arose in the execution of our plan. The Principal of St. Edmund's Hall consented without a scruple to the succession of Mr. Hill, upon my promise of continuing to superintend till he should be settled and had become a Master of Arts. Three bishops—Oxford, Hereford, and London—loaded me with civilities and kindness, and I left London on Saturday, virtually minister of St. John's. My plan is to be there in the vacations, and such times during the term as I can be spared, and to manage at Oxford till Mr. Hill is Master of Arts and of an age for holy orders, so as to be able to officiate for me in the Hall chapel and at Worton."

This letter was written in March. Somewhat later he thus reveals his motives:

"The employment of a tutor at Oxford has been far from being perfectly congenial to my mind. As to the propriety of my leaving the University, and giving myself wholly to my ministry, I cannot have a doubt. The gradual decay of vital piety in my own heart is too obvious and too alarming a symptom not to force itself upon my conscience. May God yet spare me for his honor!"

Mr. Wilson entered upon his public duties at St. John's Chapel, Bedford Row, on the 2d of July, 1809 (his birth-day), before any legal arrangement had been made, which led to a little unpleasant affair at the beginning, but his business matters were speedily arranged to the satisfaction of all parties. Two hundred guineas a year were to be paid out of the income of the chapel to Mr. Cecil and his family until the close of the lease, leaving three hundred pounds a year as Mr. Wilson's salary. To show his disinterestedness, it should be mentioned that he gave up a parish with £500 per annum, that he might devote himself more entirely to the work of the ministry.

In consequence of Mr. Cecil's long-continued illness, the congregation of St. John's had become much scattered, but within a month after the arrival of his successor, the chapel was' crowded. The building itself possessed no architectural beauties to attract, and the service was conducted in the plainest way, without any chanting—a psalm and hymn being sung, with the accompaniments of the organ. The manner of the new incumbent was natural, his voice perfect, and his action graceful and appropriate. Mr. Simeon used to say that the congregation were at his feet. The preaching of "Christ crucified" proved to be a powerful agency for arousing the slumbering consciences of the wicked, and many went away from that tabernacle humbled and penitent.

The congregation was gathered from all parts of London, and was one well calculated to draw forth the powers of a clergyman " Amongst the regular attendants were John Thornton and his sons—names suggestive of singular goodness and beneficence. There sat Charles Grant with his family, and two sons, distinguished afterwards, the one as Lord Glenelg, President of the Board of Control, and Secretary of State for the Colonies; the other as Sir Robert Grant, Governor of Bombay. There also sat Zachary Macaulay, accompanied by his son, the legislative counsellor of India and historian of England—ennobling literature, and now ennobled by it. Dr. Mason Good was there— a physician of high repute, the master of seventeen languages, and translator of the Psalms and the Book of Job, who, once a disciple of Belsham, was now 'sitting at the feet of Jesus.' Near him might be seen Mr. Stephen and his family, Mr. Cardale, Mr. Bainbridge, Mr. Wigg, Mr. Charles Bridges, and many others of high repute and piety. Lawyers of note, also, who afterwards adorned the bench, were pew-holders in St. John's. The good Bishop Ryder often attended, and Lord Calthorpe; Mr. Bowdler, the 'facile princeps,' as he was termed, of the rising barristers of his day, and Sir Digby Mackworth. Mr. Wilberforce was frequently present, with his son Samuel, 'to take care of him.' The late Duchess of Beaufort, also, often sought to hear him, with many members of her family. Individuals of every 'sort and condition' were thus assembled, high and low, rich and poor, one with another. Thirty or forty carriages might often be counted during the London season, standing in triple rows about the doors; and though there was, as is too often, unhappily, the case in proprietary chapels, but scant accommodation for the poor, yet they loved to attend, and every vacant sitting-place was filled by them the moment the doors opened."*

Many interesting incidents are related, showing the good which Mr. Wilson accomplished, while officiating as minister of St. John's. It is told of one now advanced in life, and distinguished both in the political and religious world, that when he first came up to London, to study for the bar, he casually (as men speak) entered St. John's Chapel

---
* Bateman's Life of Wilson, p. 140–1.

one Sunday evening. After standing for a long while, and failing to get a seat, he felt vexed and chafed, and was retiring. One of the settled congregation, however, saw him going, followed him to the outer door, brought him back, and made room for him in his pew. The sermon that he then heard was instrumental to his conversion, and he walked thenceforth in the way that leadeth to everlasting life. The incident is not only encouraging to ministers, but instructive to pewholders; the opening of a door may lead to the salvation of a soul.

Another incident may also be noted. A near relative of Daniel Wilson was one of a large company, when a gentleman approached and sought a personal introduction. "I wished to be introduced," he said, in explanation, "to a relative of one to whom I owe everything for time and eternity. 'I am only one of very many who do not know and never spoke to Mr. Wilson, but to whom he has been a father in Christ. He never will know, and he never ought to know, the good he has been the means of doing; for no man could bear it."

There were large Sunday schools connected with St. John's, taught by members of the congregation, which claimed the pastor's notice; and the Welsh schools, or the youth of the schools for the instruction and maintenance of children of the Principality attended upon his ministrations.

Mr. Wilson bestowed particular pains in preparing candidates for Confirmation, and on one occasion three hundred and twenty-five young persons were presented by him to the Bishop, to receive his blessing in this holy rite.

The number of communicants at St. John's was very large, five hundred being sometimes present at once, which made the service so long, that only a few minutes intervened between the close of the morning and the commencement of the afternoon service.

The collections for benevolent purposes were surpassed by those of no church in London. Mr. Wilson's appeals were most importunate, and few were able to resist them. Once, when pleading the cause of charity, he closed by saying, "Some will, I fear, notwithstanding what I have urged, pass the plate and give nothing, thinking *nobody sees.* I tell you—I tell such an one —God sees."

Although the people who attended St. John's were thoroughly evangelical in principle, they were devoted in their attachment to the Church, and when the Hon. and Rev. Baptist Noel, one of Mr. Wilson's successors, left it, for some peculiar reasons of his own, only a few individuals followed him, in spite of his great popularity.

Mr. Wilson had much to do beyond the limits of his charge, and the religious and missionary operations of the day found in him a zealous advocate and friend. During the summer holidays, having established his family at Worton, or some other country place, he made extensive tours for the benefit of the Bible or Church Missionary Society, calling forth an interest in their affairs, and collecting funds to aid them. A few incidents connected with these interesting journeys may here be appropriately introduced.

Once, when travelling with an old and beloved friend, the Rev. J. W. Cunningham, on a missionary excursion, they dined at a house where the provision was most luxurious and costly, and where a company was assembled quite foreign to the character of the deputation and their immediate object. In due course the host arose, and in a sort of uproarious manner called upon the company to drink "Health to the Deputation." The whole spirit of the dinner was offensive to devout minds, and the question was to change it. Others sat still, but Daniel Wilson rose up, and said, "I believe it is customary, when any one's health is drunk, to return thanks; and this I do most cordially; and most affectionately do I wish you, sir, in return, and this company, good health. But then (he added, in that deep tone into which his voice naturally fell when he was strongly moved) you will, perhaps, allow me to tell you in what I conceive 'Good Health' really to consist." And then he proceeded to speak of the *health of the soul*, in language so solemn and affecting that every one at the table felt the power of truth thus announced, and the whole character of the assembly was at once changed and solemnized. And yet all this was said and done with such exquisite good-humor and kindness, that not a single person was offended; but all manifested their gratitude to him in expressions of respect, almost amounting to affection.

An incident of a somewhat similar character occurred at Sir Thomas Fowell Buxton's house in town. A large party of clergy and laity, attracted by the May meetings, had been invited to his hospitable board. All were of one mind, and all desirous of mutual edification; but the evening was passing away, and the conversation was still desultory and broken. Suddenly a loud voice was heard from the top of the table, addressing one seated near the bottom. It was Daniel Wilson speaking to Dr. Marsh. "William Marsh," he said, "may I ask you a question?

You have had some experience in dealing with criminals lying under the sentence of execution; is there any portion of the Scripture that you have found more efficacious than another in bringing them to conviction of sin and true repentance? But"—checking himself, and referring to Mrs. Fry, who was sitting beside him—"perhaps I ought rather to put the question to my neighbor. May I, dear madam, ask whether any particular passage of Scripture occurs to you as having proved most useful to that class of our fellow-sinners?"

"I can have no hesitation in answering thy question," replied Mrs. Fry; "one passage I have found far more effectual than any others; and the simple reading of it has proved most useful. I refer to the latter part of the seventh chapter of Luke's Gospel. It has softened many hearts, and made eyes weep that never wept before."

"The seventh chapter of St. Luke!" said Daniel Wilson. "The latter part. Let us examine it. How glad I am that I asked you!" Then, taking a little Testament from his pocket, he began to read the passage. This led to a comment on it, to inquiries from others, and to general conversation; narratives flowed from Mrs. Fry, and illustrations of various kinds from others, so that all were pleased, instructed, and edified.

The formation of the Bible Association at Oxford was a difficult and delicate matter, in which he showed much tact. At a kind of preliminary meeting of many of the authorities of the University, he was present, endeavoring to remove objections and to win assent. The weather was oppressive, and Daniel Wilson approached one of the heads of houses, who was present, not as an approver, but a listener, with cake and wine. This gave occasion for conversation, and a hope was expressed that he would patronize the Society and take part in the meeting. An immediate refusal was given, and strong objections urged. The Society, it was said, would increase the influence of dissent, and tend so far to the injury of the Church.

"Exactly so," replied Daniel Wilson; "this will be the result if the work is left in the hands of the dissenters; and therefore, Doctor, how important it is that men of weight and influence in the Church should come forward and take the lead."

Other arguments were added, and prevailed; and thus, by his tact and good temper, he gained his point, and the Doctor became an office-bearer in the Society, and made a speech at the meeting.

Two or three more incidents may be added, as illustrating Mr. Wilson's habit and mode of prayer. A friend (the Rev. Thomas Harding, now vicar of Bexley) accompanied him to Brighton on behalf of one of the religious societies. Two large meetings had been attended; and the evening having been closed by an address to a circle of friends at Sir Thomas Bloomfield's, and by prayer, they entered the coach together on their return to town. There were no other passengers. The moment they had fairly started, Daniel Wilson, drawing up the window, said: "Now, my dear friend, we must have our evening prayers together ere we sleep." He then commended his friend, himself, and those they had just left, to the Divine protection; and, his petitions ended, he fell fast asleep.

Once, on a visit at a friend's house, he was requested to officiate at morning prayers with the family, but to be very short, because of some pressing engagement. When the servants were seated, he said: "I am requested to be very short to-day; I will therefore give you Christianity in a nut-shell. Our heavenly Father said of our blessed Redeemer, 'Thou art my beloved son, in whom I am well pleased.' Any soul that can say of that Redeemer, 'Thou art my beloved Saviour, in whom I am well pleased,' is a real Christian. Now, let us pray."

The last trait of character to be mentioned is related by Dr. Marsh, and is short and simple. He sometimes travelled, on behalf of these societies, with Daniel Wilson, and on arriving at their inn, they were frequently compelled to share a double-bedded room.

On such occasions, Dr. Marsh records the fact, that the last sight his eyes met at night, and the first sight in the morning, was always Daniel Wilson on his knees.

Such incessant and exciting labors as the zealous minister of St. John's was engaged in, could hardly fail to exhaust his strength, and we are not surprised to find that in the autumn of 1822 he was prostrate and confined to a sick room. Early the next year he resumed his public duties, but soon found that nature had not yet recovered from her previous strain; and acting upon medical advice, he made a visit to the Continent, which lasted from June to November, and which was a source of much benefit and enjoyment. He officiated on two Sundays after his return, greatly to the joy of his people, when all the bad symptoms of his disease appeared again, in even a worse form than before, and again he was compelled to learn the lessons of patience and submission, under his heavenly Father's chastening hand.

Chapter Fourth.

MR. WILSON APPEARS IN ANOTHER PULPIT—ISLINGTON—THE LAST INCUMBENT—ONE PARTY DELIGHTED, AND THE OTHER APPREHENSIVE—THE NEW VICAR'S FIRST SERMON—WAITING THE LORD'S GOOD TIME—WORLDLY WISDOM—ALL DIFFICULTIES HARMONIZED—"NO SUCH THING AS GETTING A COMFORTABLE GAME AT CARDS"—SITTING IN THE PULPIT—EFFORTS FOR ADDITIONAL CHURCH ACCOMMODATION—DIFFICULTIES IN THE WAY—THE FIRST MEETING OF THE VESTRY—A THIRD SERVICE BEGUN—IMPROVING HEALTH—CIRCULAR LETTER IN REGARD TO BUILDING NEW CHURCHES—THE FINAL ADOPTION OF THE PLAN PROPOSED—APPLICATION TO THE CHURCH COMMISSIONERS—"I AM LIKE UNTO THEM THAT DREAM"—TWO FAITHFUL CURATES—FIFTEEN SUNDAY SCHOOLS ESTABLISHED.

AFTER a silence of eight months, Mr. Wilson appeared in another pulpit, and in very different circumstances from those which had hitherto surrounded him. The important living of Islington had become vacant, and Mr. William Wilson (his wife's father having purchased the advowson,* as it is called)

---

* "Advowson is the right of patronage to a church or

presented it to his son-in-law. Although the parish was then regarded almost as a country district—green fields dividing it, in some degree, from the great metropolis—it has long since been swallowed up in the onward march of London, and all distinctive marks are swept away.

Islington was a most important charge, embracing thirty thousand souls. The last incumbent, a fine specimen of an old-fashioned divine, had been a great favorite with a large portion of the parishioners, but he had done little to rouse them from the spiritual lethargy into which they had sunk.

---

an ecclesiastical benefice; and he who has the right of advowson is called the patron of the church, from his obligation to defend the rights of the church from oppression and violence. For when lords of manors first built churches upon their own demesnes, and appointed the tithes of those manors to be paid to the officiating ministers. which before were given to the clergy in common, the lord who thus built a church, and endowed it with glebe or land, had of common right a power annexed of nominating such minister as he pleased (provided he were canonically qualified) to officiate in that church, of which he was the founder, endower, maintainer, or, in one word, the patron."—HOOK'S CHURCH DICTIONARY.

Some who had attended St. John's Chapel, Bedford Row, were residents of Islington; and these persons were delighted at the idea of having their favorite minister so near them. Others, again, expressed no little apprehension lest Mr. Wilson's thoroughly evangelical teaching and energetic manner might prove disagreeable to a congregation so long accustomed to a different system, while a few even went so far as to declare that they would not attend church.

Although still very feeble in health, the new Vicar of Islington preached his first sermon in St. Mary's Church, July 2d, 1824, entering that day on his forty-seventh year. This experiment showed him that his strength was not sufficiently restored to enable him to prosecute the work which he so much desired to begin—and he must needs abide the Lord's good pleasure. It was not until the close of November that his voice was heard again in the parish church, when he delivered a stirring Advent sermon, from St. Mark i. 15—"The time is fulfilled and the kingdom of

God is at hand. Repent ye, and believe the Gospel."

Mr. Wilson well understood the position which he occupied, and he resolved to pursue a course so prudent and unexceptionable, that while he made no compromise of the truth, none might take needless offence. Soon, however, some began to wonder at what they thought a sacrifice of principle. His appeals seemed to be less fervent, and his manner less earnest. They said, "He was very different at St. John's." They almost doubted if he preached the Gospel. But this was "their foolishness." The sermons were the same. They were St. John's sermons, wisely adapted to Islington; and the course pursued was the one most likely to produce the desired effect—"if by any means I may save some." He was gently remonstrated with by a well-wisher, and his reasons were asked. The answer was immediate, and to this effect: "I could preach away the parish church congregation in a fortnight; and in another fortnight, perhaps,

I could fill it with a congregation twice as large. But these are my parishioners. I do not wish to drive them away. I long for their souls as one that must give account. My heart's desire is to lead them to Christ. The branch in the vine must not be cut off, but made fruitful."

And his actions out of the pulpit, as well as in it, were in accordance with these words. When troublous times came on, and many were offended, some friend told him of an angry parishioner who had declared that neither he nor his family would ever come to the parish church again. "What do you say?" was the vicar's response; "what name did you mention? Where does he live? I will call on him to-morrow morning." He called accordingly, and saw the family, and all was set right in a moment; for few could resist him when he wished to please.

It is scarcely necessary to say that this action was entirely disinterested. As vicar, he was of course independent of all secular motives; and the slightest intimation of an intention of giving up a pew in church, was followed by twenty earnest applications for it. The effect of the conduct then pursued was, in the end, what he desired. None left the church; but, on the contrary, prejudices began to yield, hearts to soften, grace to work. Religion became prominent, and worldliness drew back complaining, and murmuring, "There is no such thing as getting a comfortable game at cards now, as in Dr. Strahan's time."

One old gentleman, a poor Churchman from his youth, was so full of anger at the change, that he could scarcely speak upon the subject. He threatened to leave the parish altogether. But whilst he lingered, the angel of the Lord "laid hold upon his hand," and all was changed. "No," he replied to an application about his pew, "I shall not leave. I shall remain. I find now that religion is heart-work."

It will readily be supposed that vast crowds assembled in the church, and that every standing-place was occupied.

It was the practice of the vicar now to sit in the pulpit. He was at first compelled to do this from ill health; but it became a habit, and he continued it to the end of life. A stool was constructed which would take to pieces, and which raised him, sitting, to the height of a person standing. Cross bars steadied it and rested his feet; and upon these, when excited by his subject, or desiring to impress some weighty truth upon his auditors, he often rose, greatly increasing his height, and suggesting the idea originated by John Knox, that he was about to "flee out of the pulpit." The effect, though not graceful, was impressive and earnest; and in Daniel Wilson's case, something of dignity was always attached even to his peculiarities.

When the Vicar of Islington had got fairly at work in his new parish, he began seriously to consider what arrangements could be made for additional church accommodation.

His efforts in this direction were hindered by a peculiarity in Islington—a large body of trustees, elected by the people, having power to act with the church-wardens in the management of all business matters. In consequence of this arrangement, every exciting question brought together a large crowd, and the vestry meetings were often scenes of disgraceful turmoil and confusion.

As the building of additional churches must be a work of time, Mr. Wilson wisely determined to make the best possible use of St. Mary's, and he accordingly proposed that night services should be held there, besides those of the morning and afternoon. The first vestry meeting which he presided over was called to consider this matter. He thus describes it:

"ISLINGTON, *February* 18, 1825.

"I had, last night, my vestry for nearly four hours at the church, on the evening service. About two hundred persons attended, and long discussions arose—not upon the main question, for all approved of opening the church, but on the points: Whether the church should be entirely free, or the seats be let? and then, whether the expenses should be paid by the church-wardens, or by voluntary subscription? It was carried, at length, unanimously, that the church should be free, and by 117 against 59 that the church-wardens should pay the expenses. Nothing could be more kind and respectful than their whole conduct to me, personally, but I was worn out with standing, speaking, talking, and calling to order — in short, 'ruling the waves of the sea and the tumult of the people.'"

The third service was immediately begun, and the crowded congregations were a most gratifying testimony to the expediency of such a measure. Mr. Wilson's health was improving, and his zeal kept pace with his increasing strength. Having made the best arrangement he could to supply the spiritual wants of his overgrown flock, he applied his mind to the only measure which could possibly meet the demand—the erection of new churches. The trustees were reluctant to engage in this undertaking in consequence of their unfortunate experience some years before, when a chapel-of-ease had been built. Through mismanagement, and other causes, a debt had been contracted, which still weighed heavily upon the tax-payers, and rendered them indisposed to assume additional responsibilities.

Mr. Wilson, however, prepared a circular letter to his parishioners in the spring of 1825, the main points of which were the following:

The parish contained thirty thousand people, and was rapidly increasing. Land was already let for buildings which, when completed, would raise the population to fifty thousand souls. The church and chapel-of-ease together had sittings for two thousand five hundred; so that out of every twelve parishioners, eleven were absolutely shut out of the house of God.

The trustees of the parish and His Majesty's commissioners alike concurred in the opinion that one church, in a parish spreading over so wide a surface, would be comparatively useless, and that three were absolutely required. This would involve an expense of £30,000, at the very least. But if the parishioners would find the sites, and advance £12,000, His Majesty's commissioners would take all further responsibility upon themselves, and complete the whole work. This £12,000 might be first raised, and then eventually extinguished, by a rate of three-pence in the pound, which would only require, from the great bulk of the parishioners, on an average, a payment of three or four shillings per annum—and that not from each individual, but from each family inhabiting a dwelling-house. Under certain contingencies, even this might be lessened, but it could not possibly be exceeded. And thus, at so small a sacrifice, and no subsequent risk, the whole parish might be provided with church accommodation for years to come.

The letter ended as follows:

"Let me entreat the prayers of my parishioners to Almighty God, the author of all good, that such a soundness of judgment, and such a temper of peace and charity may prevail throughout the consideration of this great question, that it may be crowned, if it should seem right and fit, with the desired success; but that, at all events, it may prove an occasion, not of heat and contention, but of good-will and kindness and conciliation between all the remotest inhabitants of this vast and important parish."

This able appeal produced a decided effect, and five days after the letter had been issued, a vestry meeting was held to consider so important a question. Mr. Wilson by no means relied upon mere human agency to accomplish the desire of his heart, but he made it the subject of unceasing prayer. And how wonderfully the Almighty overruled all things for the advancement of His own glory! The trustees assembled, and the plan proposed by the vicar was unanimously adopted. This vote, however, must be confirmed at another meeting, and although difficulties were then raised, and some objected, the previous action was approved of by large majorities.

Application must be made to the Church Commissioners, who agreed to build the churches. We give Mr. Wilson's own account:

"ISLINGTON, *May* 25, 1825.

" Surely praise should follow prayer. Yesterday our great undertaking succeeded. The two archbishops, and twenty or more bishops and noblemen, condescended to our petition, and *Three Churches*, to contain five thousand souls, are to be immediately built. The intense curiosity with which my person was surveyed by the Episcopal Commissioners is more than I can describe; and my own nervousness in answering to a thousand questions, and undergoing an hour's examination before such a Board, almost deprived me of the presence of mind necessary for such a conjuncture. To God I ascribe the whole success. I am like unto them that dream. A parish of thirty thousand people, in confusion and ill-will, and determined against any more new churches as long as they lived (we are paying £2,354 annually for our chapel-of ease), brought round to vote almost unanimously the sum of £12,000; and this pittance accepted by the Commissioners, for chapels that will cost them £35,000—and would have cost the bungling managers of a parish £70,000; this is 'the Lord's doing, and it is marvellous in our eyes.' Let May 12 and May 24 be marked in my calendar as 'jubilee days.'"

After a brief season of rest, which was passed at Cheltenham and Worton, Mr. Wilson resumed his labors at Islington, whence he thus writes on the 12th of November, 1825:

"I am wonderful well for me. In fact, I have been better the last seven weeks than I have been for years. The calls upon me since I came home have been incessant; and yet I have been able to preach at church every Sunday. The attention at church is intense. I trust and believe good is doing. The seed must have time to lie in the ground before it springs up. Oh! may the heavenly Husbandman make 'the ground' into which it falls 'good!' I begin now to find what I thought I was prepared for—checks and obstacles in my great church affairs. It is astonishing how little one is practically prepared to meet disappointments. Theory and practice are not necessarily connected in our disordered hearts."

Although nothing has been said of Mr. Wilson's assistants, our readers would hardly suppose that so much machinery could have been kept in successful operation by one man alone; but it may be well enough to mention that his efforts were ably seconded by two faithful curates—Mr. Marshall and Mr. Hambleton. Various agencies were employed for the good of the extensive parish—and among others, fifteen Sunday-schools were established—from which much precious fruit was gathered.

Chapter Fifth.

A STORM BREWING—THE AFTERNOON LECTURESHIP—A LONG AND PAINFUL STRUGGLE BROUGHT TO A PEACEABLE END—PERSUASIVE INFLUENCE—THE CROSS TAKEN UP—SEVERE AFFLICTION—MRS. WILSON'S SICKNESS AND DEATH—"THE SAME YESTERDAY, AND TO-DAY, AND FOREVER!"—RESIGNATION—LARGE CONFIRMATION —PREPARATION FOR FIRST COMMUNION—PROSPEROUS CONDITION OF THE PARISH—CONSECRATING OF THE THREE NEW CHURCHES—FREEDOM FROM DEBT—APPOINTMENT OF CLERGYMEN—THE LORD'S WORK PROSPERING.

THUS far Mr. Wilson's earnest prayer, that peace and truth might abide amongst the people of his charge, had been graciously answered. Early in 1826, however, this happy state of things was unexpectedly disturbed. The difficulty grew out of what was called the afternoon lectureship; the vicar not being responsible for this service, and about a hundred pounds a year being collected by voluntary subscriptions, to defray its expenses. The lecturer at this time was the Rev. Mr. Denham, and it was a report of his intended resignation which first suggested any disturbing question.

As the one holding this office was not obliged to perform any pastoral duties during the week, it was supposed that there might be several applicants for the vacancy, and Mr. Marshall, the senior curate, solicited the votes of the parishioners by means of a circular letter. At this stage of the proceedings, Mr. Wilson thought proper to interfere, and announced his intention, in case of a vacancy, to make arrangements himself for the afternoon service.

A controversy grew out of this—the vestry standing up for what they contended to be their rights in the case, and the vicar insisting upon his own. At the first meeting which was held on the subject, Mr. Wilson having entered a protest against any encroachment upon his privileges, promised that if the right of appointment legally belonged to the parishioners, they should be permitted to choose whom they pleased.

The vestry agreed to this, but when the vacancy really occurred, they seemed to have forgotten their engagement, and they actually met to elect Mr. Denham's successor. The motion to do this was, however, voted down, and at last, when the whole question was left to the arbitration of Dr. Lushington, it was decided in the vicar's favor.

It is grievous to think how much bitterness and ill-will had been aroused by the whole proceedings—and we are thankful to be able to record that the storm now slowly passed away. Mr. Wilson saw that it was important, for his future peace, that the influence of good and energetic laymen should be secured to modify and manage so unwieldy a body as the trustees, and he sought to interest some of his friends in this behalf. One instance will illustrate the course he pursued, and prove his persuasive influence over the minds of others. He desired to secure the services of a gentleman whose scientific attainments, courteous bearing, calmness of temperament, and general ability rendered his aid most **valuable.** With this object in view, he called upon him one morning, and said :

"I am anxious to induce the gentry of the parish, and especially those who value true religion, to take part in the management of its concerns habitually. Will you consent to be nominated as a trustee and come forward and help us?"

"I cannot think of it," was the reply. "I am a man of peace—I have my pursuits, which are pleasant to myself, and I hope, in some respects, profitable to others. I am always ready to take my part in educational matters, and in religious associations, but from parish matters I shrink."

"But I wish," said the vicar, "to urge upon you the importance of exerting your influence on the side of order, and supporting the Church and your vicar."

"And I should be glad indeed to do so. But parish business, in my view, would involve a loss of self-respect. I must decline all part in it."

"But, my dear friend, do you not believe that one day you will have to render an account to God of all the means of influence placed at your disposal, and of all the talents committed to your charge?"

"Certainly; but this is foreign to my habits and distasteful to my feelings."

"Ah! but remember, my friend, that we are called upon to 'deny ourselves,' to 'take up our cross,' to 'run with patience the race set before us.'"

"True—very true."

"Are you, then—are any of us the best judges of what is the path for us to walk in? It is not always the easy path which is the right one; it is not always when we please ourselves that we best please God. Better follow duty when it calls, and you will secure God's blessing."

The result may be anticipated. The cross was taken up, duty efficiently performed, good service rendered, a useful example set, and the great object gained.

Mr. Wilson was overtaken, in the midst

of his labors, by the heaviest trial of his life —the death of his dear, devoted wife. She had been an invalid and a sufferer for several years, and from this cause her friends had been less prepared to expect a sudden termination of her earthly course. In April, 1827, her disease grew more alarming, and early the next month it was evident to all that her end must be near. Without a murmur or regret, she turned at once to the work of self-examination, submitting herself entirely to God's holy care and keeping. On the morning of May 7th her husband entered the room, and, standing by the bedside, bent over her in silent sympathy. She opened her eyes, and recognized him at once. All the tenderness of her early love seemed to gush forth. She lifted up her wasted hands, stroked gently and repeatedly each side of his face, and whispered, "Dearest creature!" adding, "do not excite me; say something to calm me." With tearful eye and quivering lip, he named that name which is above every name—" Jesus Christ, the same yesterday, and to-day, and for ever." It found a response in the heart. "That is beautiful," she said. To her sister-in-law, who was soon after at her side, she said, "Perhaps I may not be alive long." "And if not," was the reply, "you will be in Paradise." "Ah, yes," she said, "that will be far better."

Her thoughts still clung to her children with the tenderest love. Their temporal and eternal welfare was very near her heart; and when all was silent in the room, her voice was often heard ascending up to heaven in earnest supplications on their behalf.

"My dearest love," said her husband, on coming in, "you will soon be with Jesus." "*To see Him!*" was her brief but weighty answer.

Soon the power of articulation began to fail, and the notice of external things to lessen. All stood around the bed—husband, children, sisters, servants. She noticed no external thing, but still held communion with her God. "Lord, have mercy on my soul! Succor me in Jesus Christ. In sickness and in dying, oh, succor and save! Lord, let me enjoy Thy presence for evermore. I have no merits in myself, but my reliance is on Christ. Lord, save me in Christ Jesus. I do love Him. Though I am a sinner, save me for His sake."

These were the last connected words. A few fragments only of love and piety could afterwards be gathered. "Lord, teach submission"—"no more sin"—"sing with joy"—"dear John"—"dear Dan"—"resignation"—"*Saviour!*"

Till the afternoon of Thursday death lingered; and on that day, May 10th, at one o'clock, she ceased to breathe, and her spirit returned to that Father who gave, and that Saviour who redeemed it. She slept in Jesus; whilst friends knelt round her bed, weeping, yet sorrowing "not as others who have no hope." She was interred in the family vault under the parish church of Islington. The funeral sermon was preached by the Dean of Salisbury; and then the bereaved husband set out once more on the journey of life, a solitary and widowed man. He had lost one who had been a help meet for him—his counsellor in difficulties, his comforter in sorrows, his nurse in sickness. He never ceased to think of her with true affection, nor to speak of her with tender regret.

"Indeed, it is all true," was the expression of his first letter after the event; "I have lost the companion of my youth, the partner of my joys and sorrows, the mother of my children, the guide of my Christian course. My sorrows flow deeply, and must flow, so long as I remain behind. But I hope I do not murmur. I hope I desire to say, 'Not my will, but Thine be done.' I hope I am grateful for four-and-twenty years of peace, and union, and comfort. I hope I bless God for the delightful testimony to her Saviour which she bore in life and death."

Although Mr. Wilson was greatly distressed by this late affliction, he regarded it as a call from God, requiring him to be more devoted in His service.

Almost seven hundred young persons in his parish had just renewed the vows of Baptism in Confirmation, and he was now most anxious to prepare them for their first Communion. Besides preaching on the subject, he urged them to come to him, in private, for additional instruction, and many gladly availed themselves of the privilege.

The year 1828 found the affairs of the parish in a most encouraging state. In addition to three full services on Sundays and great festivals, the church was opened for prayers on every Wednesday and Friday morning, and on Saints' days.

The next important event to be noted is the consecration of the three new churches, which had been erected within the bounds of the parish.

St. John's Church, Holloway, which accommodates about eighteen hundred persons, was consecrated by Dr. Howley, then Bishop of London, on the 2d of July, 1828, and St. Paul's, at Ball's Pond, on the 23d of October, in the same year. This church is about as large as St. John's. Trinity—the largest of the three, having two thousand and nine sittings—was consecrated on the 19th of March, 1829.

The whole business arrangements had been so admirably managed that, so far from contracting any debt, a balance of one hundred pounds was returned to the parish. Mr. Wilson presented to each church on the day of its consecration a beautiful communion set. His great anxiety was to secure efficient clergymen for them, and after due consideration, the Rev. W. Marshall, the Rev. John Sandys, and the Rev. H. F. Fell were appointed. The churches were soon filled, and the work of the Lord prospered. The good vicar continued to feel the deepest interest in them until his dying day.

Chapter Sixty.

THE PRIVATE JOURNAL ONCE MORE RESUMED—MR. WILSON'S ENTRANCE UPON HIS FIFTY-THIRD YEAR—HONEST CONFESSIONS OF A CONTRITE HEART—ISLINGTON IN AN UPROAR—CAUSE OF THE DISTURBANCE—THE PRAYER OF FAITH RECEIVES AN ANSWER OF PEACE—A VOICE FROM INDIA—DEATH OF BISHOP TURNER—DIFFICULTY IN FINDING A SUCCESSOR—MR. WILSON OFFERS TO GO—HIS MOTIVES SCRUTINIZED—CONSECRATION—PREPARATIONS FOR LEAVING ENGLAND—SETS SAIL FOR CALCUTTA.

WE have now brought down our narrative to the year 1830. On the 12th of January, Mr. Wilson takes out his old private note-book once more, and makes this record: "Twenty-three years have passed since I wrote in this journal. I can scarcely say why—I believe that I ceased to write because pride gradually increased, and I could not even describe the state of my soul without some inflation, which spoiled all."

Again, on the first of July, he writes in this journal, in which the secret workings of his heart are described: "To-morrow, if it please God, I shall complete my fifty-second year, and enter my fifty-third. What should be my resolutions for the new year? Tell me, O my soul! what I ought to do, as it respects my private devotions, my ministerial work, my children, religious societies, and the Church of God.

"1. My private devotions ought to be more regular, fervent, and spiritual—above all, I ought to study the Bible more humbly and prayerfully.

"2. My ministry demands more simplicity, sweetness, tenderness of heart, spirituality, fidelity, boldness.

"3. My children require my prayers, my example, my instructions, and a steady, consistent walk.

"4. The societies need carefulness to avoid divisions, and to keep from needless interference; all must be open, straightforward, wise.

"5. The Church of God wants a heart full of charity, a single eye, and the simplicity of Jesus Christ in all things.

"I have, myself, to guard against (1) pride: (2) the lusts of the flesh; (3) vain and worldly reading. Give me, O God! the needful grace."

Once more, on the 10th of the same month, we find these honest confessions of a contrite heart. "How can I begin my meditation! How can I enter Thy presence, my God! My thoughts oppress me. The instability of my character, the weakness of my will, my frequent relapses, shut my mouth and make me miserable. I have preached this morning on the fall of David, from the words, '*Thou art the man.*' But I have more need of self-application than any of my hearers.

"'I am the man!' the man unfaithful, the man ungrateful, the man proud, the man living to himself—the man full of covetousness, weakness, and corruption. O my God! have pity on me. Visit me with Thy grace. Give me Thy Spirit. Destroy in me the dominion of sin, and set up the kingdom of purity and virtue."

About the time that Mr. Wilson was

making these entries, all Islington was in an uproar. The difficulty arose from an unintentional error which had been made in the election of the parish trustees, for which he was in no way responsible. It gave occasion, however, for the old spirit of opposition to show itself again, and several stormy vestry meetings were held. The vicar's friends were unwilling that he should be exposed to the thickest of the contest, and the senior warden presided in his place. We shall not attempt to go into particulars, but merely say that the agitated waves of party strife ere long subsided, and when the warden, in his capacity of chairman, went to the vicar to report, the latter replied to his congratulations on the favorable result:

"My dear sir, I thought it would be even as you had said, because I knew that God heareth and answereth prayer. The moment you left me last night, I sent for my curates, that 'two or three' might agree in what they should ask; and when you were taking the chair, we fell upon our knees and besought the Lord to give you a mouth and wisdom that no adversary might be able to gainsay or resist. Thus, whilst you were striving in the plain, we were praying on the mount. And this is the result. May God be praised!"

"Ah, sir," said the church-warden, when giving this account of his vicar, with tearful eye and quivering lip, "ah, sir, he was indeed a man of prayer."

Mr. Wilson had spent eight years at Islington, and thirty thousand persons had felt the influence of his devotion to their service.

It had seemed a great undertaking when he entered upon the care of this single parish, but it was as nothing compared with that which now awaited him.

In 1831, Bishop Turner, of Calcutta, died. He was the fourth prelate who, within a short space of time, had sunk under the enervating climate of India.

It is curious to observe how Mr. Wilson's thoughts had for years past been turned towards the East. His interest in Bishop Heber we have already referred to. In 1829, when

Dr. Turner was about to sail for his distant diocese, he visited Islington, and attended a meeting of the Church Missionary Society. Mr. Wilson presided, and in his address he assured the Bishop that if, at any time, the people of Islington could give or do anything to benefit India, they were ready. Little did he foresee how that pledge would be redeemed!

Bishop Turner had so great confidence in Mr. Wilson's judgment, that he begged him to make such suggestions as he thought would be of use to him in his Indian Episcopate—which request was faithfully complied with.

Two years passed by, and Bishop Turner had been taken away, and India was calling for another to fill his place. Such a fatality had attended those who had hitherto gone out (four Bishops having died within nine years), that several who had been offered the mitre, declined to accept it. In this emergency, Mr. Wilson declared his willingness to go, in case no one else could be found.

Does not the death of his devoted wife seem designed by Providence to break a tie which might have bound him fast to England, and kept him back from long years of service in India? Let no man presume to say that it was ambition which prompted the Vicar of Islington to make the proposal he did. He was most happily situated, enjoyed an ample competency, occupied a high position, was surrounded by loving friends, and exercised a wide influence. What could India offer in exchange for these? Those to whom the appointing power was entrusted, were sensible of the deep responsibility which rested on them, and they made the most anxious inquiries concerning Mr. Wilson's fitness for so difficult and trying a position. All were at last fully satisfied that he was well qualified for the office, and he was accordingly offered the Bishopric of India. No further time was to be lost. Nine months had already passed since the death of Bishop Turner, and his successor should be ready to depart.

Sunday, April 29th, was fixed for the consecration. On that day he arose early, and made this entry in his journal: "I am now come to the beginning of this awful, solemn, delightful day—the day of my espousals to Christ my Saviour—the day of my renewal of my vows as deacon and priest, and of the additional vows of superintendent, overseer, and Bishop of the Church of Calcutta. O Lord! assist me in the preparation for this office. Aid me during the solemnities of the day. Grant me grace after it to fulfil my engagements and promises."

At prayers with his family that morning, he expounded St. Paul's address to the elders of the Church at Ephesus, and with deep feeling and faltering voice applied some of the verses to his own case.

"I also go to India under somewhat similar circumstances with the Apostle; in that 'I know not the things that shall befall me there.' But his God will be my God, and his Father my Father, and therefore none of these things move me."

The consecration took place in the chapel of Lambeth Palace, the Archbishop of Canterbury being assisted in the solemn office by Dr. Bloomfield, Bishop of London, Dr. Monk, Bishop of Gloucester, and Dr. Gray, Bishop of Bristol.

The new bishop of Calcutta reached home about five in the afternoon, and retiring to his study, appeared no more that day. The following were his evening meditations: "Lord, I would now adore Thee for Thy great grace given unto me; that I should be called to the office of Chief Pastor and Bishop of Thy Church. Oh! guard me from the spiritual dangers to which I am most exposed—pride, self-consequence, worldliness of spirit, false dignity, human applause, abuse of authority, reliance on past knowledge or experience. Lord, give me simplicity of heart, boldness, steadiness, decision of character, deadness of affection to the world. Let me remember that the great vital points of religion are the main things to be kept constantly and steadily on my heart, then compassion for souls, then simplicity of object, and abstraction from every other interfering claim; then a spirit of prayer and supplication; then learning lessons from affliction, when God sends it."

We shall not attempt to describe the multiplied engagements which occupied his last days in England. Having seen his son inducted into the living of Islington, and attended to every other duty, he left his native shores on the 19th of June, 1832, in the ship *James Sibbald*, bound for Calcutta.

Chapter Seventh.

MAKING GOOD USE OF A SEA-VOYAGE—DAILY ROUTINE ON SHIP-BOARD—INTERESTING LETTER TO THE DEAN OF SALISBURY—THE DARK AND BRIGHT SIDES OF THE PICTURE—DESIRE TO GLORIFY GOD—ARRIVAL AT CAPE TOWN—AN UNEXPECTED VISITOR—TEN DAYS WELL SPENT—AFFECTING FAREWELL—MORE DILIGENT THAN BEFORE—SICKNESS BREAKS OUT—FIRST SIGHT OF INDIA—LANDING AT CALCUTTA.

ANY one who has experienced the inconveniences and discomforts of a sea-voyage, will be prepared to give Bishop Wilson full credit for his efforts to be useful during so trying a period. The confinement of the ship, to a certain extent, affected his health, but he made the best use of his time, as will be seen from the following extract from a letter to a friend:

"*July* 26, 1832.

"We live very regularly. My day is this: I rise at six o'clock, and spend till nearly eight in my cabin; then walk for a quarter of an hour before prayers in the cuddy, when I read and comment on the prophet Isaiah; reading and writing, with occasional walks of five minutes interposed, occupy the morning till two o'clock; we dine at three; repose in cabin follows till five; at half-past five we have evening prayers on deck, when I read and comment on the Acts of the Apostles; tea at six; then come exercise and reading; at nine o'clock, private prayer in cabin, with my daughter and chaplain; at ten o'clock I am in my cot, with light put out. Our provision is abundant. There were shipped, I understand, thirty-six dozen of poultry, forty sheep, forty pigs, one hundred barrels of beer, one hundred and fifty Yorkshire hams, and a cow to give milk all the voyage; besides dried fruits, preserved meats, and wines, including champagne and claret."

A letter to the Dean of Salisbury, which we transcribe, will interest our readers and furnish the best account of his experiences on the great deep.

"*Saturday, July* 28, 1832. N. Lat. 4° 10′, W. Long. 14° 12′, about 4,300 miles from England by the log, and 400 miles from Cape Palmas.

"Did you ever see such a date, with so many guides to the reader? But such is the best method of giving you a correct notion of our present spot. We are hoping to meet some homeward-bound vessel as we pass the line, and I write in order to avail myself of the opportunity. We have had a most favorable passage thus far—not very quick, but most agreeable; no storms, no heat, no calm, no rain. We are now entering the trade-winds, which will not leave us, as we hope, till we reach the Cape. The sea-sickness was a mere trifle; in one week we had overcome it. But the real pressure upon the mind and body is separation, the severing of all bonds of nature and habit, desolation of heart, the feeling of being alone and imprisoned on the wild, barren, boundless ocean, without the possibility of escape; no change, no external world, no news, no communication. Then, the difference of diet, bad water, bad butter, bad tea, a rolling cot by night and an uneasy ship by day, the head confined, the heart withered, the capacity of thought and prayer lost! These constitute the privations of a five or six months' voyage, undertaken for the first time, in the fifty-fourth year of a minister's age, and after all his habits and associations have been buttressed and propped up by parish committees, public duties, a circle of brethren, and the endearments of a family.

"This is the dark side of the picture. Reverse it, and all is brightness, joy, confidence in God, peace, anticipation, gratitude for being permitted to enter on such a design, and preparation for a future day. And all the previous chaos of feeling has its lesson. It constitutes a 'dispensation,' and draws one inward upon conscience, faith, prayer. These allure the heart out of itself, and, from the sensible objects of discouragement, to God and His sovereignty, omnipresence, all-sufficiency, and then it arrives at peace, its true felicity and end. I have been much reflecting on the mysterious course of events which have led me to this cabin as a Bishop of India, compared with my education as a boy destined for commerce, in December, 1792. Then began that intercourse with my father-in-law, which led to my espousing his eldest daughter in 1803, to the parish of Islington, to the new churches, and from these to Calcutta. When I trace back this order of events, I am smitten with adoration at the mercy and compassion of the Lord. If a single link had been wanting in the chain, the whole would have fallen to pieces. Yes, my beloved friend, I look back, like Jacob, to the time when with my staff I passed Jordan, and now I am become two bands. To the Lord only be all the praise ascribed. My heart overflows with love and adoration to my God and Saviour for all His mercies. And yet other feelings perhaps surpass these —a sense of *humiliation* for my returns for all these benefits. I cannot enter upon this topic, it would defeat its object. But God knoweth my heart. What a sinner before my practical knowledge of the Gospel, and what a feeble, wandering soul since! One more thought, however, equals, or ought to equal, this—the desire to glorify God, and fulfil my duties in the *Superintendence* and *Bishopric*, now so unexpectedly entrusted to me. All my past history should make me the more anxious to amend, to rise higher, to acquire more wisdom, to act with more decision, promptitude, disinterestedness, and consistency; to believe, love, and obey, with more elevated and aspiring motives than ever. Nothing more easy than to mar the last scene of life. But to fill it up with dignity, meekness, discretion, holiness, simplicity of aim—this is the difficulty. Lord, help me!"

It had been arranged, previously to Bishop Wilson's departure from England, that he should stop at the Cape of Good Hope, and discharge such Episcopal functions as might be required, notice having been sent beforehand to that effect.

When the vessel reached Cape Town, he was sorry to find that these despatches had not been received, and no preparations made for his visit.

The Bishop was, however, received with the utmost courtesy by the Governor, and arrangements were made to enable him to spend the brief period of his sojourn to the best advantage. Besides preaching on several occasions, visiting the schools, consecrating two pieces of ground on which churches were to be built, attending a meeting of the Society for Promoting Christian Knowledge, and holding an ordination, he confirmed three hundred persons. An affecting farewell address closed his labors at Cape Town—when many followed him to the ship, and with tears and prayers for his safety, bade him good-bye. The ten days, thus profitably spent, were long remembered with satisfaction and delight by the inhabitants of the Cape, and the Bishop found in them a useful preparation for the more arduous duties which awaited him. During the remainder of the voyage he diligently applied himself to his studies, drew closer to the missionaries and catechists, who were his fellow-passengers, and began a course of lectures in his private cabin, in anticipation of the ordination at Calcutta.

Meanwhile, sickness had broken out, the Bishop's daughter being one of the sufferers. It was a great relief to his anxious mind when they reached the yellow waters of Sangor—and, in due time, the low mud banks of the Hooghly presented themselves to view.

When the ship cast anchor off Kedgeree, a little steamer came alongside, bringing Archdeacon Corrie and Dr. Mill—the former of whom, having long known the Bishop, now hastened forward, embraced, and kissed him, with the most tender affection. The James Sibbald was towed by the steamer to Calcutta, where the Bishop landed, under a salute from the fort, on Monday, November 5th, 1832.

Chapter Eighth.

THE BISHOP'S INSTALLATION—KIND ADDRESS TO THE CLERGY—JURISDICTION OF THE BISHOP OF CALCUTTA IN 1832—A WISE DIVISION OF SO VAST A FIELD—FIRST SERMON IN THE CATHEDRAL—GENERAL INSPECTION OF SCHOOLS AND MISSIONARY SOCIETIES—THE CIVILITIES OF LIFE — BISHOP'S PALACE — "ENOUGH FOR SIX MONTHS!"—MARRIAGE OF A DAUGHTER—TWO YEARS FOR ACCLIMATION—IMPOSSIBILITY OF PLEASING EVERYBODY—WISDOM JUSTIFIED OF HER CHILDREN—PERSONAL HABITS—MODES OF GAINING INFORMATION—FRIENDLY AND CONFIDENTIAL INTERCOURSE WITH THE GOVERNOR-GENERAL — ATTENDING TO BUSINESS ON HORSEBACK—"LORD WILLIAM IS LESS OF A CHURCHMAN THAN I COULD DESIRE."

THE same morning that Bishop Wilson landed at Calcutta, he went to the cathedral, where he was installed* by Archdeacon Corrie, with the usual ceremonies, about twenty clergymen being present. He took advantage of this occasion to make a short

---

* A full description of the service of installation will be found in the Life of Bishop Stewart, of Quebec, in this series, p. 94.

and affectionate address, in which he begged an interest in their prayers, and assured them that he wished to be regarded as a brother to the older clergy, and a father to the younger.

The jurisdiction of the Bishop of Calcutta, in 1832, extended over territories now wisely divided into sixteen distinct dioceses. The burden was enough to crush any one who should make the attempt to carry it, and yet the new prelate of India was resolved, by God's help, to do what he could. So little had hitherto been accomplished in the way of establishing great general principles of action, that he was obliged to proceed with extreme caution, taking advice from others, and calling his own good sense into constant requisition.

On the 11th of November, the Bishop preached his first sermon in the cathedral, choosing for his theme the language of St. Paul [Ephesians iii. 8], "The unsearchable riches of Christ." A large and attentive congregation, including the public authorities, was in attendance.

He next went round preaching in all the other churches in Calcutta and the neighborhood. He also visited Bishop's College and the several mission schools, presided over meetings of the Societies for Promoting Christian Knowledge, and for the Propagation of the Gospel, besides writing letters of instruction to Madras, Bombay, Ceylon, Australia, and China.

All this while the whole society of Calcutta was paying him the courtesies due to his position and office, and he was busy making arrangements for taking possession of the house which the Government provided for his use. This was entirely unfurnished, and when the Bishop first went to see it, he found such a scanty supply of chairs and tables scattered through it, that he said to Archdeacon Corrie, to whom he had written from England to have it provided with all things needful, "Why is this?" The good clergyman replied, "I thought, my lord, that there was enough to last for six months." As most of the Bishop's predecessors had died within this brief space, he concluded, in his simplicity, that it would be foolish to make arrangements for a longer period. The Bishop smiled, but immediately gave orders to have the house completely furnished. India was henceforth to be his home, and, in order to prolong his days for usefulness, he must secure for himself the comforts of life.

Before the close of the year 1832, the Bishop's daughter became the wife of his chaplain—the Rev. Josiah Bateman—a marriage which gave great satisfaction to the devoted father. The new comers had been advised to remain for two years in Calcutta, in order to become acclimated, and they followed these prudent counsels.

It is impossible for a man to please everybody, let him act as wisely and prudently as he may. Bishop Wilson soon found that Calcutta was like Jerusalem of old. "There were children sitting in the market-place, and calling one to another, and saying, 'We have piped unto you, and ye have not danced; we have mourned to you, and ye have not wept.'" Bishop Heber had been blamed for neglecting etiquette; Bishop Wilson was blamed for observing it. Bishop Turner had been censured for keeping no establishment, seeing little society, being little known, and failing, consequently, in acquiring that influence which he had often needed in carrying out his wise and practical measures. Bishop Wilson was accused of ostentation for keeping open house, for using hospitality, and for acquiring in this way valuable friends and extensive influence.

But wisdom is justified of all her children. His personal habits at this time were very simple and regular. He rose early, and rode on a small black horse, brought from the Cape, which for a time was able to take care both of itself and its master, and by an easy amble gave air without effort. Private devotions were succeeded by family prayers in the chapel which he had himself fitted up. His chaplain, from the reading-desk, read the appointed lesson, and he, from his seat, expounded it, and then prayed. A hearty breakfast of rice, fish, and soojee (a kind of porridge) followed. The morning was then given to business. At mid-day he rested, and generally slept for two hours; and though business went on, he was never disturbed. Refreshed by sleep, he was ready for the afternoon dâk, and for any matters that pressed for decision. The evening ride or drive and the late dinner followed; family prayers and evening devotions closed the day. Good appetite and sound sleep, the two pillars of good health, sustained him during the many years of his Indian course.

He was indefatigable in acquiring information. Every chaplain as he visited the Presidency, each missionary when he called on business, travellers like Dr. Wolff from far countries, all civil and military servants with whom he came in contact, were put under contribution. No pains were spared, no opinion despised, no advice rejected. A visit to Dr. Carey at Serampore elicited many interesting reminiscences of the early Christianity of India. A visit to Russipugla gave reality to the missionary work now carrying on. A friendly conversation with Dr. Duff furnished important information on the subject of native education. All was written down at the time in a MS. book, and preserved for future perusal, enlargement, or correction. He was, in truth, thoroughly a man of business. His heart was in his work. It engrossed even his morning ride and evening drive. When others, weary with a sleepless night or breathless day, sought the early bracing air or cool evening breeze, and felt totally unfit for business, he seemed fit for nothing else, and to like nothing half so well. Join him, and the business of yesterday, the plans of to-day, the prospects for to morrow, were instantly brought upon the tapis; and the matters discussed already many times, were discussed at full length once more. It was thus he developed his ideas and fixed his purposes. His mind was cleared and made up, not so much by thought as by conversation. The repetition caused him no weariness. Business was his recreation and delight.*

When Bishop Wilson first reached Calcutta, he was received by the Vice-President, attended by his aides-de-camp; the Governor-General, Lord Bentinck, being then absent on a tour through the upper provinces. The Governor-General, however, sent him a courteous greeting, and after returning to Calcutta in February, 1833, he called on the Bishop without ceremony, and friendly and confidential intercourse at once began. They were accustomed to go out on horseback together almost daily, and much important business was transacted during these pleasant rides.

"Lord and Lady William," says the Bishop, when writing to Mr. Charles Grant, "are a blessing to India. We differ widely about establishments, etc., but what is that compared to a difference, which might easily occur, about the good of India, the interests

---

* Bateman, p. 252, etc. Many passages taken in whole or in part from this work, are not specially noted.

of the natives, and the diffusion of Christianity, on which we are strongly agreed?"

And again, later: "Lord William is rather more of a Whig, and less of a Churchman, than I could desire, but incomparably better than the highest Churchman, if without piety, vigor, and activity. Lord William reverences religion and its sincere professors and ministers, but he has prejudices against bishops, ecclesiastical establishments, and national churches."

Chapter Ninth.

DETAILS OF LABOR—DIFFICULTIES IN THE FREE SCHOOL, AND MEASURES TAKEN TO RECONCILE THEM—PUBLICATION OF PAINE'S "AGE OF REASON"—LECTURES ON THE EVIDENCES OF CHRISTIANITY — CLERICAL MEETINGS—THEIR EFFECTS—BISHOP'S COLLEGE—THE NEW BISHOP DOES HIS DUTY AS A VISITOR—FIRST ORDINATION IN INDIA—A HOLY WEEK—LARGE CONFIRMATION—THE "SEVEN DUTIES"—NOT TOO LATE—AN AWKWARD INTERRUPTION—CONVERSION OF THE NATIVES—THE BISHOP VISITS AN INTERESTING MISSION—CHRISTIANITY AND PAGANISM SIDE BY SIDE—BAPTISM ADMINISTERED—"GOOD, GOOD."

THE two years spent by Bishop Wilson in Calcutta, while becoming accustomed to the enervating effects of the climate, were very busy ones. We must go somewhat into details, in order to show the multiplicity and importance of his engagements.

The FREE SCHOOL—a noble institution, founded many years before, for the benefit of the East Indian and Portuguese inhabitants of the city, where three or four hundred children were trained for future usefulness—had been much hindered in its great mission for good, by unhappy dissensions among the trustees.

At the urgent request of all parties, the Bishop consented to arbitrate in the matter. Having made himself fully acquainted with all the particulars of the case, he brought his worldly wisdom to bear upon it, and at last succeeded so perfectly in restoring harmony and peace, that he received a cordial vote of thanks for his kind and conciliating conduct. All this was to him a subject of grateful praise, as every previous step had been a subject of fervent prayer.

Infidelity had been active in India, as in other quarters of the globe, in attempting to sow tares among the wheat; and on the Bishop's arrival, a copy of Paine's "Age of Reason" was handed him—one of a large edition which had been published by some who professed to be Christians, for the perversion of the educated and inquiring natives. In order to counteract the evil effects of this dangerous book, he delivered a course of Lent Lectures, in the cathedral, on the Evidences of Christianity, which were largely attended, and produced a very decided impression.

One of the Bishop's first acts was to establish a series of clerical meetings, to be held at his own house, with a view to cultivate more friendly relations among the clergy of Calcutta and the neighborhood. Personal friendships were thus strengthened and prejudices removed, many interesting theological questions were discussed, and devout prayers offered up for the influences of the Holy Spirit, which we may believe were abundantly answered. The Bishop always opened the discussion himself, after having given a brief statement of measures in progress, or completed, for the benefit of the diocese. Each clergyman present was called upon in turn to express his opinion, and at the hour of prayer all proceeded to the chapel, to make known their wants unto God, and to implore the great Head of the Church to bless the labors of His servants.

In 1832, although the buildings of Bishop's College were complete, and the institution was in operation, the pupils were few and the prospects discouraging. According to the statutes of the College, the Bishop of Calcutta was made a visitor, by virtue of his office—all pecuniary arrangements being supposed to be sanctioned by him; and yet so many unpleasant difficulties had arisen between the College authorities and Bishop Turner, that he had quietly withdrawn from all interference. His more energetic successor felt that this would be wrong, and he accordingly resumed the position which lawfully belonged to him, and by a course at once kind and decided, he did much to promote the usefulness of this noble institution.

Bishop Wilson's first ordination, in India, was held on the Epiphany after his arrival, when two candidates were admitted to the holy order of Deacons, and seven to the Priesthood. As all subsequent ordinations were conducted after the same model, it will be proper to mention that during the week preceding the solemn occasion, the candidates were guests at the Episcopal palace—lectures being delivered, each day, at morning prayers, from one of the Epistles to Timothy or Titus, of which notes were taken down by those for whose benefit they were delivered. And thus the whole week was spent in prayer, examination, and in familiar instructions—a week which was never forgotten.

On Tuesday, April 2d, 1832, the Bishop held his first Confirmation in India. Four hundred and seventy persons appeared in the cathedral, and participated in the sacred rite. Of these, more than one hundred were native Christians. Their numbers excited great astonishment at the time, and no small apprehension as to the effect upon those that were "without." They clustered round the communion rails, whilst the Europeans filled the body of the cathedral. The services were read, and the rite administered separately.

The many confirmations following this

first, seemed always to be attended with a blessing. The Bishop's manner was most impressive, and his words most earnest and affecting. He usually gave two addresses—one, hortatory, before the administration, and one, practical, after it. The full assent of the catechumens he almost always required to be repeated twice, and sometimes thrice, till the church resounded with the words, "I do." And in the second address, he was accustomed to deliver seven rules, which were to be repeated after him at the time, and written in the Bible or the Prayerbook afterwards. Subsequently they were expanded and printed; but originally they were short and sententious, as follows:

1. Pray every day of your life for more and more of God's Holy Spirit.

2. Prepare at once for receiving aright the Holy Sacrament of the Body and Blood of Christ.

3. Read every day some portion of God's Holy Word.

4. Reverence and observe the Lord's Day.

5. Keep in the unity of the Church.

6. Avoid bad company, and seek the company of the good.

7. When you have got wrong, confess it, and get right as soon as you can.

In many a Bible and Prayer-book throughout India these words will be found written; by many a civilian, soldier, East Indian, and native Christian have they been repeated and treasured up. "Please, sir, will you give us our seven duties," was the constant request to the Bishop's chaplain after service. A copy of them was always made, and left behind at every station, for the use of those who had been confirmed. Many interesting, and some curious, incidents occurred in connection with them, of which the following are specimens:

On one occasion, when the Confirmation was concluded in a large military station, and the Bishop was resting for a few minutes in the vestry, a young and noble-looking English soldier hastily entered, and made his military salute. On being questioned, it appeared that he had been a candidate for Confirmation, and was duly prepared; but, having been on guard, he was too late for the ceremony, and came now to express his sorrow, and see if his case admitted of a remedy. For awhile the Bishop doubted; but his interest was roused by hearing the soldier plead previous knowledge, and say that he had been a boy in the Islington parochial schools; that he had often been catechised in that church, and that he had heard the Bishop's last sermon.

"Kneel down," said the Bishop. He knelt, and was confirmed, and admitted to the full communion of the Church militant on earth.

On another occasion, in the Straits, when the Bishop was enumerating these seven duties, and requiring the assent and pledge of the catechumens to observe them, a voice was heard from the midst refusing compliance. An aged man had been confirmed, of an eccentric character. "No," he said, "he would observe what the rubric required, but would pledge himself to nothing more." No difficulty, of course, was made; and with the surprise the matter passed away. It was not the time or place to dwell upon " all those things which your godfathers and godmothers then undertook for you."

The conversion of the natives to the true faith was a subject in which the Bishop felt the deepest interest, and whenever any missionaries had candidates ready for Baptism, he was glad to give the sanction of his presence.

On Whitsunday, 1833, he baptized a native convert, who had passed through the various stages between the dark regions of heathenism and the purer atmosphere of the Gospel. Afterwards, we find him going in a flat-bottomed boat, hollowed out of a tree, to visit the missions of the Society for the Propagation of the Gospel, under the charge of the Rev. D. Jones, and his catechist, Mr. Driburg. When the little church-bell rang out its cheerful invitation to assemble for public worship, the beating of the tomtom in a pagan temple hard by seemed to breathe defiance.

After Divine service, the candidates for Baptism were publicly examined, and the Bishop admitted seven to the ark of Christ's Church, and then addressed them in an impressive discourse from our Saviour's words, "I am the light of the world," each sentence being translated by the missionary. Great interest was manifested, and now and then a low murmur was heard of "good, good;" "true, true;" "yes, yes."

During the first two years of the Bishop's residence in Calcutta he witnessed the baptism of one hundred and seventy-eight natives—a number which was afterwards largely increased.

Chapter Tenth.

UNHAPPY DIVISIONS AMONG CHRISTIANS A HINDRANCE TO THE GOSPEL — BISHOP WILSON DISCOURAGES A SPIRIT OF PROSELYTING—ESTABLISHMENT OF INFANT SCHOOLS—SUCCESSFUL EXPERIMENT—EXTRACT FROM A BENGALEE PAPER—THE BISHOP'S EFFORTS IN BEHALF OF STEAM NAVIGATION BETWEEN ENGLAND AND INDIA—THE WIDE SPACE BRIDGED OVER BY ORIENTAL STEAMERS—RENEWAL OF THE EAST INDIA COMPANY'S CHARTER — THE KING AUTHORIZED TO MAKE SOME IMPORTANT CHANGES IN CHURCH AFFAIRS—BISHOP WILSON'S JOY AT THE DAWN OF BETTER DAYS—THE DIOCESES FILLED, AND THE NEW MACHINERY SET TO WORK.

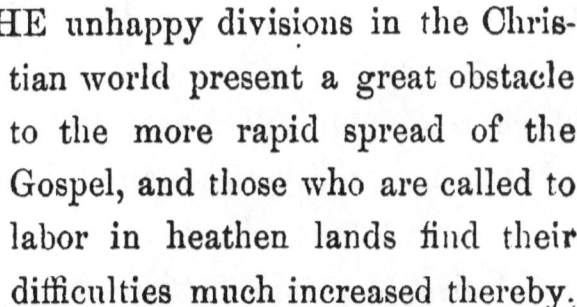

THE unhappy divisions in the Christian world present a great obstacle to the more rapid spread of the Gospel, and those who are called to labor in heathen lands find their difficulties much increased thereby. Not only are the poor benighted pagans perplexed by the disputes among the disciples of one Lord and Master, but the missionaries of different denominations often expend more energy in battling with each other, than in waging war against the common enemy of all.

Bishop Wilson thought, as the field was so broad, that it was inexpedient to encourage any thing like the proselyting of native Christians from other Protestant bodies—not only because it would occasion much hard feeling among the missionaries, but because it might encourage persons who had been disgraced in one congregation to seek refuge in another. Much could be said on both sides of such a question, and it is one about which good men will conscientiously differ.

It had been a favorite plan with the Bishop to establish infant schools in India, as being an admirable means for developing the native mind and character. Having interested a number of influential men in the enterprise, a subscription was raised of five thousand rupees, and a competent master and mistress sent for from England. The school was first opened, in 1834, for the benefit of the nominally Christian children of Portuguese and East Indian descent, and every thing promised well. The Bishop presided at a public examination which was held in the Town Hall, in June of the following year, many influential natives being present, and expressing themselves as greatly delighted with the exercises.

It was now determined to open a school for native children, to be under the care of the same master and mistress as the other school, but in a distinct apartment. In four months' time, an examination of native children, from two to seven years of age, was held, a large audience having assembled to witness it. One hundred native infants, clad in the splendid dresses of the East, and decked with the ornaments of the harem, crowded the platform, and went through all the exercises usually displayed at home. They spoke English fluently, sang hymns, marched, clapped hands, examined one another, showed wonderful intelligence, and elicited universal admiration. No infant school in England could have surpassed these little bright-eyed, dark-skinned Indians. The experiment completely answered. The European gentry were charmed; and the feeling amongst the natives, generally, may be judged of by an extract from a Bengalee newspaper published at the time. Thus spake the editor of the Gyananeshum:

"On Thursday morning a meeting of the Infant School Society was held in the Town Hall. The Lord Bishop, Sir Edward Ryan, Sir Benjamin Malkin, Sir J. Grant, Lady Ryan, and numerous other friends of education, of both sexes, were present. After the business of the Society had been transacted, the boys of the native infant school were ushered in. They were about a hundred in number. The postures they put themselves into, at the command of their master, were pretty and amusing. They sang several English songs, and kept clapping the time in good order. They astonished the audience by the expertness with which they answered questions put to them in numeration, addition, the tables of currency in this country, etc. All this was done, in English, by the

Hindoo children. The audience seemed to be much gratified at their progress. The Lord Bishop took particular notice of the correctness of their pronunciation, which he highly eulogized."

The experiment having proved a complete success, the Bishop was anxious to have such schools established throughout India, and application was made to the "Education Committee" of the government to provide funds for the purpose. The Committee received the proposition with many gracious words, and for three years nothing was done on the subject. Meanwhile the native school in Calcutta continued to prosper, but another generation may pass away before the many advantages of such institutions will be enjoyed throughout the widely extended boundaries of India.

But it was not only in religious and educational matters that the Bishop exerted himself for the benefit of society. Among other subjects which engaged his attention was that of steam communication between England and her distant provinces in the East. In 1832 it was not uncommon for a letter to be one hundred and seventy or eighty days on the voyage, a most unfortunate delay for those engaged in business, and most painful to kindred and friends living at such a distance apart.

Bishop Wilson felt that by shortening the long intervals of correspondence, the general interests of India would be materially promoted, and the Gospel extended under more favorable auspices. The subject had been talked about for some time, and here it seemed likely to end, until he came to the assistance of those most nearly interested, when a feasible plan of operations was immediately prepared and permanent steps taken. It was unusual, indeed, to see a bishop presiding over a public meeting where such questions were discussed, but his rare gifts of energy and decision, tempered by prudence and common sense, were too much needed at such a time to permit him to remain inactive. He did not cease to exert himself in the cause until the distance between England and India was bridged, as it were, by those splendid Oriental steamers which have done so much to soften the necessary pains of absence, and to insure, in cases of danger, earnest sympathy and prompt relief.

In October, 1833, tidings reached India that a bill had been brought into Parliament for the renewal of the East India Company's charter, which also empowered the king to divide the diocese, to erect Calcutta into a metropolitan see, and to appoint two suffragan bishops for Madras and Bombay. While Bishop Wilson was ready to shrink back at the bare thought of the responsibilities which would thus be laid upon him, his heart overflowed with thankfulness at the brightening prospects of the Church.

"How can I tell you my joy at the prospect of the suffragan bishops!" he says, in a letter to an old friend. "How I labored that plan before I left England, in June, 1832! The president, the chairman, the

Archbishop, the Bishop of London, the secretary of the Board—all were assailed and urged by me in turns. The two Mr. Grants at first thought the whole plan impracticable, but ended (after three months' incessant drives, and comparisons of plans, and references, and delays) in the arrangement of a bill, drawn by Mr. Groom, the solicitor of the Board.

"Well do I remember Mr. Simeon saying, that if I had been made Bishop of Calcutta merely to carry that measure, and was never to reach India, I should have done a great work. My disappointment, of course, was the more keen when Dr. Dealtry sent me word last August that it had been found impracticable to bring in the bill that session; for on the Saturday, June 16th, when I dined at Mr. Grant's, the first thing Earl Grey had said, upon my being introduced to him, was, that he highly approved of the measure as circulated by Mr. Grant, and thought it very reasonable. I then went up to the Bishop of London, and with joy brought him to the

Prime Minister, when he confirmed what he before had said. This took me to Mr. Grant and to the chairman, to express my gratitude and delight. I conceived, in fact, that the thing was carried, and *so it was;* for now it is inserted in the charter speech, not as a matter of debate, but as previously arranged; and probably the very bill drawn and ready in June, 1832, will be passed now. And how greatly are my joy and gratitude to Providence enhanced by the very delay and disappointment! Mr. Grant's speech came upon me as a thunder-stroke. I wrote off instantly a long letter under the first impulse of joy. I have now heard from Dr. Dealtry (June 23) to know my wishes as to the men. I have proposed Archdeacon Corrie for Madras, Archdeacon Robinson for Bombay, and Archdeacon Carr, now of Bombay, to be, by my appointment, Archdeacon of Calcutta, instead of Corrie.

"I am advising Corrie to proceed to England instanter for consecration, and I propose to meet him, on his return, at Madras, and consecrate (if we are permitted) Robinson.

"My soul swells with thanksgivings and praise to God for his vast mercy, not as it respects my Episcopate, but the permanent good of India. But I fear even to write to you of these feelings, lest I should grieve the Holy Comforter; for Satan's grand assault upon my mind since March 27th, 1832, is elation, joy, natural spirits, eager pursuit of a great object, a soul panting to stretch itself to the length and breadth of my vast diocese."

The bill passed Parliament August 21st, 1833, and reached India at the close of the year. Considerable delay occurred in carrying out its provisions; for the expenditure sanctioned for the whole ecclesiastical establishment was limited, and the Archdeaconry of Bombay being filled up, as we have seen, the funds did not at once admit of the appointment of both bishops. Eventually, however, all came round. Archdeacon Corrie—one of those men whose praise is in all the churches, and whom the Bishop deemed, for meekness and gentleness of spirit, more like his Divine Master than any one he had ever known—was recalled from the visitation on which, with proper allowances, now for the first time obtained, he had been engaged, and sent to England. He returned, in 1835, Bishop of Madras. The Archdeacon of Madras retired on his pension. Archdeacon Carr was summoned home in 1837, and returned Bishop of Bombay.

All the dioceses were then filled, and a new machinery began to work. It formed a precedent of vast importance for a spreading church, and has been followed, both in Australia and in Africa. They also have now their metropolitans and suffragans ; and if ever, in the providence of God, these great dependencies are separated from the parent stock, their Church will still retain within itself the power of reproduction and indefinite expansion—still be enabled to put forth great branches, and bear fruit for the healing of the nations.

Chapter Eleventh.

THE WANT OF SUITABLE PLACES FOR PUBLIC WORSHIP—
A FEASIBLE PLAN FOR REMEDYING THE EVIL—ITS
GRATIFYING RESULTS—A KNOTTY QUESTION WHICH LED
TO SOME DIFFICULTIES—THE BISHOP LOSES CONFIDENCE
IN PUBLIC MEN—PREPARATIONS FOR A VISITATION OF
HIS DIOCESE—HIS FIRST CHARGE TO THE CLERGY—
DEPARTURE FOR PENANG—WHAT HAPPENED THERE—
A FLOURISHING NUTMEG PLANTATION, AND ITS CLERICAL OWNER—AN AMUSING INCIDENT—ARRIVAL AT
SINGAPORE—ITS RELIGIOUS DESTITUTION—SOME IMPORTANT STEPS TAKEN—PRESBYTERIAN SCRUPLES REMOVED.

THE want of suitable buildings for public worship had long been felt in India, and the barrack and the ball-room had been the only places which could be secured for the purpose. No regular plan for remedying the evil was proposed until 1834, when a communication appeared in the *Christian Intelligencer* (then edited in Calcutta by Bishop Wilson's chaplain and son-in-law), suggesting that a fund should be raised, by voluntary subscriptions throughout India, of one rupee a month—the management of the fund being vested in the Bishop, Archdeacon, and Presidency chaplain.

This plan, with some modifications, was speedily carried into effect, and its results may be gathered from a brief extract from a report published in 1857: "There are now one hundred and twenty churches in this diocese (Calcutta), including those in the course of erection; and to sixty-six of these has this 'One-Rupee-Subscription Fund' contributed, since its commencement in 1834, sums amounting to eighty-one thousand seven hundred and thirty-eight rupees."

During all the time which had elapsed since the Bishop's coming to India, we must imagine him taking exercise every morning on horseback, usually in company with Lord William, and discussing important questions of Church and State, as usual. The relation of the chaplains to the Government and the

Bishop was one of these, and it had caused no little disturbance and anxiety.

Having been formally requested by the Government to define the duties of chaplains at military stations, and to give his opinion as to the degree of authority which it was proper for the commanding officer to exercise at such stations, he acceded to the request according to his best judgment, the Governor-General fully agreeing with him in his decision. And yet, strange to say, when Lord William published his official orders, not long afterwards, he took entirely different ground. The Bishop could hardly believe his eyes when he read the paper, but after having appealed, in several able letters, from the decision which had been made, he submitted as patiently as he could. Few understood how deeply his feelings had been wounded, and how much his confidence in public men had been impaired. His private notes, however, make some disclosures. He thus writes:

"If, after consulting a bishop as to the

relative position of military officers and chaplains, and agreeing solemnly with the explanations given, the Government can then publish orders in contradiction to that explanation, and their own avowed pledge of concurrence; if they do this without informing the Bishop; if they do it after having communicated other points of difference, but concealed this, what can a bishop do or hope for? Where is faith or trustworthiness to be found?

"But, hush, my soul! Silence thy human reasonings and carnal complaints! This is Thy hand, O my God! and Thou, Lord, hast done it. Is it not by Thy permission, and for the spiritual humiliation of the Christian, that the events of this world take place? Before Thy righteousness I desire to bow, trusting that Thou canst reverse these evils, if for our real and highest good, and believing that Thou art calling on us to cease from man and creature props, and to rest ourselves entirely and unreservedly on THY ALMIGHTY ARM."

The climate of India and the pressure of business were producing their effect upon the Bishop's health, and he was by no means sorry when the two years were ended, and he could enter upon a visitation of his extensive diocese. The serious illness of his daughter, which rendered a sea voyage indispensable, increased his anxiety to leave Calcutta, and he accordingly requested that a vessel might be provided for conveying himself and his suite to the various settlements on the eastern coast, and thence across the Bay of Bengal to Madras and Ceylon.

The primary visitation was held in the cathedral, at Calcutta, on the 13th of August, 1834, twenty-one clergymen being present, when the Bishop delivered his charge, which had occupied his attention for several months past. When his reverend brethren gathered about him, he commenced his address by saying, "That in the short space of twelve or thirteen years a fifth bishop of Calcutta should be addressing his reverend brethren from this chair, is a most affecting memorial of the uncertainty of life, and of the mysteries of the Divine judgments. As to man, all is weakness and change. The pastoral staff drops from the hand before it is grasped. Measures are broken off in the midst; and we must look to the mercy of God alone for the settlement and future safety of our apostolical branch of Christ's holy Catholic Church in India." His feelings were overpowering; all the circumstances connecting together the past and the present seemed to rush upon his mind; his voice faltered; he paused in deep emotion, and was a considerable time ere he could resume his self-command. Then, continuing his address, he riveted the attention of all his hearers, and sympathy gave place to a feeling of deep solemnity.

The statistical part of the address showed a considerable improvement in Church affairs in India.

After the close of this interesting assembly, the Bishop delivered a farewell sermon at the cathedral, and early on Monday morning,

August 24th, he embarked, under the usual salute, and went forth on his first visitation. The passage to Penang was prolonged by adverse winds, and was rendered more anxious by the continued ill health of his daughter; but on the 19th of September the vessel glided into the roadstead formed by the island of Penang on the one side, and the Queda Country on the other.

The Bishop and his party landed immediately, and were hospitably received and sheltered in the house of Sir Benjamin Malkin, the Judge and Recorder of the Straits. Nothing could exceed the kindness manifested by himself and his excellent lady during the whole of the Bishop's stay; and after he left, his daughter, having derived no benefit from the sea voyage, and being unable to continue it, found there a home for many months, and remained until increasing illness compelled a permanent return to England.

The real business of the visitation soon began, and all that could be done the Bishop did. The chaplain was first visited in his parsonage, and the Bishop looked grave when he found attached to it a flourishing nutmeg plantation. Words of caution only were spoken now, but the pursuit was afterwards forbidden.

The colonel in command at the station, wishing to show the Bishop all possible respect, proposed that the troops should pass in review before him, which was accordingly done. This is rather amusing to think of, but it was meant in kindness, and it was so received. Having visited the schools and hospitals, preached three times, confirmed forty-eight persons, and administered the Lord's Supper, he took his leave and embarked for Singapore. This is a free port, to which merchants of all nations had access, and the place had neither been famed for morality nor honesty. As no church had hitherto been built, and religious services were not celebrated with any regularity, the Bishop was very desirous to take prompt measures for establishing a better state of things. He landed on Saturday night, and sent around notice of Divine service and the Holy Communion for the following morning, and of a public meeting for Monday. The attendance on the Sunday service was large, and all the influential people in the settlement met on Monday morning, to discuss the propriety of building a church. The Bishop presided, by their request, and submitted a plan for raising funds, which was speedily adopted, and three thousand dollars were subscribed before the adjournment of the meeting.

The young persons who were desirous of Confirmation were then called together, and examined and instructed. A good many of them having been brought up Presbyterians, had some objection to the reference in the preface to the Confirmation office to godfathers and godmothers. The Bishop decided that, in all such cases, the natural parents stood to their children in God's stead; and that this being previously understood and allowed on both sides, they might answer conscientiously, and he confirm willingly.

He then addressed them earnestly upon the point of dedication to God, and on the appointed day administered the rite.

Having consecrated the church-yard, and encouraged the building committee to go on with their work, the first Episcopal visit ever paid to Singapore was brought to a close.

Chapter Twelfth.

MALACCA CAUGHT NAPPING—RESULT OF THE BISHOP'S VISITATION—MOULMEIN—YELLOW ROBES AND SHAVEN HEADS—HOPEFUL PROSPECTS—SPICY BREEZES FROM CEYLON—THREE WEEKS OF CONSTANT LABOR—DANGEROUS PASSAGE TO MADRAS—NARROW ESCAPE FROM SHIPWRECK—AN ESPECIAL ERRAND, AND NOT A PLEASANT ONE—THE CASTE QUESTION—NO MORE HALF-WAY MEASURES—WINNOWING THE CHAFF FROM THE WHEAT—TIME-SERVING POLICY OF THE GOVERNMENT—PROCEEDS TO TANJORE—"THE TRACK OF THE HOLY AND BELOVED HEBER"—RECEPTION AT TANJORE—THE OLD NATIVE PRIEST—SECRET ASPIRATIONS.

ON the night of October 10th Bishop Wilson landed at Malacca, and sought shelter in the old white Stadt-house, no one being there to welcome or to entertain him. "From the sublime to the ridiculous there is but a step," he said, with great good-humor, as he seated himself upon an empty box; and the next morning, with his usual energy, all necessary arrangements for the visitation were made. Divine service was celebrated in the old

Dutch church, which the trustees kindly offered to transfer to the Bishop if he would consecrate it, and secure the appointment of a chaplain. He promised to do his best to obtain a clergyman for them, appointed a candidate for Holy Orders, as lay-reader, but deferred the consecration of the building until a chaplain had been sent. Twenty-nine were confirmed, and thirty-one communicated; and after bidding the people an affectionate farewell, he writes home in regard to Malacca:

"God grant that the spices and fragrance of grace and holiness may equal the exquisite odors of this place. But one feels horrified to think that we are in the midst of pirates, murderers, and opium eaters—men of fierce and barbarous usages beyond conception. Oh, what would not Christianity do for these poor creatures! It is a comfort to think that the rule of England is merciful and beneficial compared with that of the Malays, Mohammedans, Portuguese, or even the Dutch, imperfect as our Government is.

May the spirit of real piety and zeal fill our rulers more and more! I am sure the Bishop has enough to do, as well as the clergy, in beginning every thing aright."

The steamer now turned her course towards Moulmein, and here it occurs to me to recommend the reader to open a map of Asia, and follow the Bishop in his journeyings.

All was new and strange in Moulmein, which was part of the territory ceded to the English in the last war. Pagan priests with flowing yellow robes and shaven heads were numerous, and idols of gigantic size sat in the temples which had been erected for their worship. A large body of English troops were then stationed in Moulmein, and many distinguished officers.

Mr. Hamilton, the chaplain, assisted in making arrangements for the Bishop's visitation, which included an inspection of the schools and hospitals, the consecration of a handsome Gothic church, and the administration of the rite of the "Laying On of

Hands." On the 28th of October the Bishop took his leave.

"I have been finishing," he says, "the last Sunday of my second year's residence in India by preaching my hundred and fifty-second sermon, before five or six hundred persons of all ranks, in the newly consecrated church of Moulmein. It is a beautiful structure, just such as Augustine built in England at the conversion of the larger cities towards the end of the sixth century. We have been proclaiming the Gospel in the Burman Empire, with China on one side and India on the other; Bhûd and his monstrous fables deceiving four hundred millions on our right; and Brahma with his metaphysical atheism chaining down one hundred millions on our left; whilst the base impostor Mohammed rages against the Deity and Sacrifice of the blessed Saviour in the midst of both, with ten or twenty millions of followers. But our DIVINE LORD shall ere long reign; and Bhûddist, and Brahminist, and Mohammedan—yea, the infidel, and papist, and nominal Christian throughout Asia, shall unite in adoring His cross."

On the 7th of November the Bishop was regaled with the sweet breezes from the cinnamon groves of Ceylon, and a new and beautiful scene was unveiled before him. But he had something to do besides inhaling fragrant odors and admiring lovely scenery. Many urgent matters pressed for settlement, misunderstandings between the highest authorities of Church and State must be examined into; disunion among the clergy must be healed; learned controversies in regard to two different versions of the Bible into Cingalese must be listened to, and a final decision made—all this, and more, came upon the Bishop at the very beginning of his visitation. He exercised a sound discretion in the settlement of every difficulty, and if all parties were not satisfied, none could censure him for showing an undue bias to either side.

On Sunday, he preached to an overflowing congregation, in the Fort church, and on

Tuesday confirmed one hundred and eight young persons, the words and final blessing being repeated in English, Cingalese, Portuguese, and Tamul.

On Tuesday the Bishop held his visitation and delivered his charge to the clergy. These multiplied engagements were varied by a visit to the Church Missionary Institution at Cotta, which he thus describes: "I must tell you of the exquisite drive we have had through the cinnamon gardens for five miles. Nothing since the garden of Eden was so beautiful—a vast field of green fragrant bush, with every fibre and branch bursting with cinnamon. But even this extraordinary scene yields to the moral fragrance of this dear missionary station of Cotta, now numbering twelve out-stations, four clergymen, twenty-one native teachers, six hundred average attendants on public worship, twenty-one communicants, nineteen seminarists, sixteen schools, and four hundred and thirty scholars. Our honored Mr. Lambrick, after eighteen years of steady and holy labor, presides over the whole. Will you believe that I have been examining native youth in the English Scriptures, geography, history, astronomy, mathematics, Latin, Greek, and Hebrew?"

Fifty-five young natives were confirmed here. Having made an excursion to Kandy, the ancient capital of the island, where Bhûddism was seen in one of its strongholds, and a faithful missionary was cheered in the midst of discouraging labors, the Bishop returned to Colombo on the 18th of November, in time to examine the candidates for Holy Orders. Three days afterwards, the ordination was held, and soon he was under way for Matura and Trincomalee. At the latter place, the visitation of Ceylon ended, having cost three weeks of incessant labor.

In his passage to Madras, the Bishop barely escaped from death, through the mercy of Him who can rule the raging of the sea. The condition of the poor, worn-out vessel was so perilous, that the captain cried out in despair, " I can do no more; tell the Bishop he had better go to prayers." Almost overcome with fatigue and sea-sickness, the good man obeyed the summons, and having read St. Paul's account of his shipwreck (Acts xxvii. 13–36), his voice being well-nigh drowned by the groaning of the ship and the noise of the waves, he called upon the Lord to deliver them. The Almighty, who hears the supplications of His servants, made the storm to cease.

At day-dawn, December 10th, they landed at Madras. The Bishop had come here on an especial errand, and he had looked forward with much anxiety to the results of this visit. "The Caste question" had been the occasion of many difficulties in this portion of the missionary field, and it was concerning these that prompt measures were now to be taken.

We can only explain, very briefly, that while in Bengal, and elsewhere, the natives who embraced Christianity had been obliged to give up all connection with idolatry and its usages, greater liberty had improperly been granted to the converts in Southern India, which had allowed half the evils of Paganism to be retained under the name of Christianity. The old distinctions of caste were so far preserved as to mar the solemnities of public worship, and to engender envy, hatred, and pride—and all this had been winked at for years, lest any interference on the part of the missionaries should alienate large numbers of their congregations.

Bishop Wilson was well informed in regard to these things, and rejecting all timid counsels and time-serving compromises, he looked at the question simply as a matter of right or wrong, and acted accordingly. In the summer of 1833 he addressed an earnest letter on the subject to the missionaries throughout his diocese, in the course of which he takes the following decided positions:

"1. The catechumens preparing for baptism must be informed by you of the Bishop's decision, and must be gently and tenderly advised to submit to it. Of course, the minister informs the Bishop or Archdeacon a week previously to the intended baptism of each convert, agreeably to the directions given by my honored predecessor, in his charge delivered at Madras, in November, 1830; and this will afford opportunity for each particular case being well considered.

"2. The children of native Christians will, in the next place, not be admitted to the Holy Communion without this renunciation of castes; their previous education being directed duly to this, amongst other duties of the Christian religion, no material difficulties will, as I trust, arise here.

"3. With respect to the adult Christians already admitted to the Holy Communion, I should recommend that their prejudices and habits be so far consulted as not to insist on an open, direct renunciation of caste. The execution of the award in the case of all new converts and communicants will speedily wear out the practice.

"4. In the mean time, it may suffice that

overt acts, which spring from the distinction of castes, be at once and finally discontinued in the church: whether places in the church be concerned, or the manner of approach to the Lord's table, or processions in marriages, or marks on the forehead made with paint or mixtures, or differences of food and dress— whatever be the overt acts, they must, in the church, and so far as the influence of ministers goes, be at once abandoned."

The circulation of this letter produced a great sensation. Many of the native converts went back to their old ways, and congregations which had been large and flourishing were suddenly reduced to a mere handful. It was a thorough winnowing of the chaff from the wheat. The Bishop was duly informed of all that occurred, and his advice was freely given in all cases of perplexity. His difficulties were greatly increased by the cowardly policy of the Government, which was disposed to yield to the remonstrances of the natives, and to suffer matters to fall back into their former state. Surely, England paid dearly, at a more recent day, for her unfaithfulness towards India, and her countless children sunk in ignorance and degradation!

Bishop Wilson was not a man to falter in the discharge of a plain duty, and he was determined to abide by the decision which he had given. While he remained at Madras, he delivered sixteen sermons and addresses, confirmed six hundred and seventeen, and delivered his charge to the clergy, besides attending several committee meetings of different religious bodies. He also preached twice in the church of the native Christians of Vepery; and although to all outward appearances a stranger would have been well pleased with their orderly and reverent behavior, one more familiar with them could not fail to have observed the old distinction of caste in as active operation as before. The Bishop concluded to do nothing more to restrain this evil until his return from Tanjore. Towards that place he now hastened, treading in the steps of his predecessor, and accompanied by Archdeacon Robinson, whose society was as pleasant as his experience was valuable. Madras was left on December 29th, and on the 31st, at Atcherawauk, the following words were written:

"Our ten miles' march is over, out of which I rode four on my Pegu pony. The close of another year calls to consideration of the end of life, usefulness, projects, designs. The track of the holy and beloved Heber is solemn and affecting indeed. Poor fellow! The thermometer, as he journeyed, sometimes stood at 112 degrees; and even in his tent, the Archdeacon who accompanied him says they could not get it lower than 97 degrees. It was the very worst season of the year for the south (March to April, 1826). Sir Thomas Monro again and again warned him that the end of January was the last moment he should have left Madras. God's holy will, however, is thus accomplished in us and in the Church. Two things striké me: (1) Bishop Heber's sudden death was necessary to seal his doctrine, to awaken all India, to turn his astonishing popularity and loveableness into an attachment to the cause in which he died, to fix England and India in one gaze of interest. (2) His death, after two and a half years of residence and journeys, saved him all the odium, misrepresentation, conflict with the worldly, envy of the wicked, and jarring with religious societies. All was thus *couleur de rose;* and as to influence after his decease, he died at the exact moment."

Early on the morning of the 10th of January, 1835, the Bishop espied the pagodas of Tanjore; and at a ford over one of the branches of the river Cavery a large number of native Christians and school-children were assembled. The venerable missionary Kohlhoff was at their head, and crowds of heathen stood around. The river was soon crossed, and the Bishop immediately alighted from his palanquin; but before he could salute them, a hymn of praise rose on the morning air, sounding most sweet from native tongues. When it was ended, mutual greetings were interchanged. The native priest Nyanapragasen (the effulgence of glory), eighty-three years of age, drew near and was presented. His long white robe, combining in one garment both gown and cassock, harmonized well with the snowy hair falling on his shoulders, and gave him a most venerable appearance. He took the Bishop's offered hand between both of his, and blessed God for bringing him amongst them, adding a hope, that as Elijah brought back the stiffnecked Israelites to God, so he might overcome the obstinacy of this people.

After a few more kind words, the Bishop bade them farewell, and hastened on to the Residency, where Colonel Macleane and his admirable family were ready to receive and entertain him.

"Here I am, entering into this once flourishing Church, O Lord, in Thy name, and with a single eye to Thy glory and the purity of Thy Gospel over all India. Grant me Thy meekness, Thy wisdom, Thy firmness, Thy fortitude, Thy discretion, Thine address in treating with men. To Thee do I look up. As to myself and human power, my heart faileth me. For what can I do with seventeen hundred revolters and ten thousand uninformed and prejudiced Christians? Lord, undertake for me."

Such were the first secret aspirations of his soul. We must leave further particulars for the next chapter.

Chapter Thirteenth.

MOST UNPROMISING CONDITION OF AFFAIRS—LOOKING TO GOD FOR HELP—SWARTZ'S GRAVE—INTERESTING SERVICES—EFFORTS TO BRING THE NATIVE CHRISTIANS TO A BETTER MIND—JOURNEY TO TRICHINOPOLY—SERVICES IN THE MISSION CHURCH—BISHOP HEBER—THE CASTE QUESTION AGAIN—MEETING THE DIFFICULTY BOLDLY—SOME CHANGES FOR THE BETTER—ORDINATION AT TANJORE—A RALLYING POINT GAINED—HAPPY SIX MONTHS—SAFE ARRIVAL AT CALCUTTA.

AFFAIRS at Tanjore were in a most unsettled condition. Large numbers of native Christians had refused to submit to the Bishop's decision in regard to forsaking their old pagan rules of caste, and the state of morals was deplorable. The missionaries had become extremely unpopular, and every thing was as unpromising as it well could be. Refuge was sought in God, as the only hope, and the Bishop prayed most earnestly that he might be guided to do what was for the real good of the Church. Having held several conferences with some of the native priests, catechists, and others, he invited them all to attend service on Sunday, and they promised to do so, if they could sit according to their former arrangement of caste. Permission was given them, on this occasion, to follow their own inclinations.

On Sunday, the Bishop preached in the morning to the English congregation. Divine service was held in the Mission church—a hallowed spot, where Swartz and other venerable men had ministered through life, and found a resting-place at death; where many souls, rescued from heathenism, had been added unto the Lord; and where some of Heber's last loving words had been spoken.

In the evening, from the same place, the native Christians were addressed. The service, necessarily, was in Tamul, and young Mr. Commerer, who was a catechist, and spoke it admirably, acted as the Bishop's interpreter. Seven hundred and fifty persons were counted, sitting, after their manner, on the floor of the church, of whom more than three hundred were **Soodra** men and women; whilst uncounted crowds stood round the doors and windows.

The Bishop's text was, " Walk in love, as Christ also loved us;" and he dwelt upon two points—the love of Christ to us, and our love to one another. He was very affectionate and very earnest, and the effect was perceptible, the whole congregation was moved. Towards the conclusion, he dwelt upon the character of the " Good Samaritan," as illustrative of the love we should bear to one another. He described the meeting with the " certain man" of the parable; the seeing him in distress; not asking him who he was; not dreaming of defilement by contact with him; but meeting the present duty; pouring in oil and wine; putting him on his own beast; taking care of him; and all because he was in distress, **and because he was a neighbor.**

" And what," asked the Bishop, rising from his seat, and with outstretched arms bending over the congregation which sat beneath him, "what did our blessed Master and Saviour say concerning this? What was his doctrine? What was his command? What were his words? Go AND DO THOU LIKEWISE!"

A long pause of motionless and breathless silence followed, broken only when he besought every one present to offer up this prayer: "Lord, give me a broken heart, to receive the love of Christ and obey his commands." Whilst the whole congregation were repeating these words aloud in Tamul, he bowed upon the cushion, doubtless entreating help from God, and then dismissed them with his blessing.

On Monday the Mission churches and buildings were inspected; the room in which Swartz died, and all the other places of interest, were visited; and then another conference was held, at which it was resolved to invite all native Christians, who might wish it, to private conversation, affording thus an opportunity to hear their difficulties, and help in their removal. Time would fail us to give even an outline of all the efforts which were made to bring the unhappy people to a better mind The native Christians were in sore perplexity. They had hoped that the Bishop would yield to their importunities, but they found him both kinder and firmer than they expected. On the 21st of January he set out for Trichinopoly, proposing to defer any final arrangements until his return. Stopping at a large native station, called Multoopatty, he preached, and administered the holy Sacrament to two hundred and forty-seven native communicants, no foolish question of caste troubling any mind. In the afternoon, sixteen children were baptized.

"Never," says the Bishop, recalling this day, "had I such grace given me since I have been in orders, now thirty-four years, as is now vouchsafed; that I, who am, indeed, 'less than the least of all saints,' should be permitted to preach amongst the Gentiles 'the unsearchable riches of Christ.' If God carries me through this series of duties and labors, I may say truly, 'Lord, now lettest Thou Thy servant depart in peace, for mine eyes have seen Thy salvation.' One such day as we have just passed is worth years of common service. I really almost wish I might resign Calcutta, and take the see of Madras. These native churches require just the care I should delight to give."

On Friday, January 23d, he reached Trichinopoly, a place of fifty thousand inhabitants, where the beloved Heber died.

Here, the troublesome caste question was again encountered. The Bishop preached in the Mission church on the day after his arrival, taking no notice of the Soodras, who were clustering together in a group by themselves, and who had not been near the church for nine-months before. They had a native priest amongst them, and he, as well as many of the congregation, being possessed of independent property, were apparently determined to stand out. It was necessary, however, that the matter should be at once brought to an issue, for the

Bishop had but a few days to stay, and he would return no more.

Here, therefore, he resolved, for the first time, to carry out the purpose he had formed. There was no hope that, in any case, the whole dissentient body would comply with his wishes. The evil lay too deep, the prejudices and habits were too strong. But a nucleus might be formed, round which others might gather from time to time, and to which all new converts might be added. If this nucleus could be formed in each station, and arranged upon the basis of the Bishop's direction, then time, patience, and watchfulness, by God's grace, would do the rest.

This, therefore, was the Bishop's purpose; and to accomplish it, notice was given of Divine service and the administration of the Lord's Supper, for the very morning of his departure. All seemed impressed with the importance of the occasion, and the church was thronged. When the Bishop, in his robes, left the vestry in order to proceed to his seat at the communion-table and commence the service, he saw many scattered groups of natives standing apart from the main body of the congregation, who were seated on the floor. Fully aware of the cause, he joined one group, and taking two native Christians by the hand, he gently led them forward to a vacant place in front, and seated them. His chaplain, following in the surplice, by his directions, did the same. Others who were present were bid to assist. It was all done quietly, and no sort of resistance was made. The Soodra sat by the Pariah, and the Pariah by the Soodra, and both were intentionally intermingled with many of the authorities and influential Europeans of the station.

When all was quiet, the service commenced; and in the course of it forty natives came up, without distinction, and were confirmed. Then followed the sermon, from the words, "Preaching peace by Jesus Christ." When the holy Sacrament was about to be celebrated, the Bishop quietly gave directions as to the mode of administration. A Soodra catechist received it first, then two Pariah catechists, then a European gentleman, then a Soodra, then some East Indians. The gentry of the station, having been much interested in the matter, had placed themselves at the Bishop's disposal; and, at the special request of the lady of the highest rank, a Pariah knelt and communicated between her and her husband. This facilitated the arrangement; and silently, but most effectually, the barrier which had existed for so long a time was broken down, and one hundred and forty-seven partook of the Lord's Supper, without distinction.

A precedent was thus set. This was the nucleus of the native Church of the future. Every wanderer, every dissentient, might join it; but always in this way and according to this rule. New converts also, and every one who was confirmed, would know what was expected from them. Dead leaves would gradually drop off; these were to be the new buds.

Of course many Soodras had retired from the church before the Sacrament was administered, and all had been free to do so. But it was found that nine families of influence had conformed, and were well content. These, with the large body of Pariahs, were sufficient for the purpose; and the Bishop thanked God and took courage. He preached once more, and made a collection, which Bishop Heber's death had prevented his doing nine years before, for the Propagation Society, and then took his departure. He called at the missionary station of Boodalore, in his way, and arrived at Tanjore again on Wednesday morning, January 28th.*

Three days after his return, the Bishop held an ordination, when four deacons were admitted to the priesthood, and a Lutheran missionary was made deacon. The next morning was appointed for service with the natives, and as it was the last time he could meet them, it was anticipated with some

---

* Bateman, p. 381-2.

anxiety. The day began auspiciously by the receipt of a letter from the native Christians at Vepery, signed by seven, in the name and on behalf of all, confessing past errors, and promising unfeigned and unconditional obedience for the future.

The morning prayers were read in Tamul at eight o'clock; and at half-past ten all were assembled for the sermon and holy Sacrament. They arranged themselves as they pleased; a few sat apart; but the greater number were mingled together. About six hundred were present. The Bishop did not interfere, as at Trichinopoly. After the Litany, he preached from the words, "Why are ye fearful, O ye of little faith?" The whole congregation seemed to remain for the holy Sacrament; for though some had retired, yet the church looked full. The Resident and ladies of his family first approached—then some Soodras and Pariahs intermingled—then some Europeans—then natives and Europeans mingled—then natives and East Indians mingled—then one or two missionaries and natives. All was voluntary, and all was perfectly understood.

The only remaining peculiarity—and that was fairly allowable, and perhaps desirable—was, that amongst the natives men and women communicated separately—the men first, the women after. The whole number of communicants on this occasion was three hundred and forty-eight. Of these, sixty-two were Europeans, and two hundred and eighty-six native Christians, amongst whom forty-three were Soodras from Tanjore and the neighborhood. Here, again, God gave success. The number thus conforming certainly was small, as compared with the many non-conformists; but it was sufficient for a precedent. It afforded a rallying point; and the Bishop was content.

The result was better than at one time he anticipated. Henceforth all depended on strengthening the mission, watching over new converts, and instructing the rising generation.

Having delivered his "Missionary Charge"

at Tanjore, the Bishop retraced his steps to Madras, where he arrived on the 14th of February, 1835, "having spent," he says, "the happiest six months in my life; so much do I love missionary work." Ten days were given to Madras, and by the 2d of March he was once more safely sheltered beneath his own roof, in Calcutta, having completed a journey of six thousand five hundred miles.

Chapter Fourteenth.

AT HOME, BUT NOT IDLE—CHANGE IN THE GOVERNMENT, AND THE DEPARTURE OF FRIENDS — AN AFFECTING DUTY—LORD WILLIAM RETURNS HOME—PERPLEXING QUESTIONS SETTLED—THE BISHOP RESUMES HIS VISITATION—ENTRANCE-GATE TO THE SYRIAN CHURCHES—BRIEF ACCOUNT OF THEM—SERVICES AT QUILON—SETS OUT FOR THE INTERIOR—PREACHES AT ALLEPIE—ATTEMPTS TO BENEFIT THE SYRIAN CHRISTIANS—THE COLLEGE AT COTTAYAM — BISHOP WILSON WAITED UPON BY THE SYRIAN CLERGY—HIS CONFERENCES WITH THEM—"NEVER AGAIN SHALL I BEHOLD SUCH A SIGHT."

ALTHOUGH Bishop Wilson had reached home, it was not for the enjoyment of rest. The atmosphere of Calcutta was foggy, damp, hot, and suffocating; but he roused himself up to bear the pressure of daily duties, and many perplexing cares. Changes were soon to take place in the government, friends were departing for England, and his own faith seemed sometimes almost to waver. Lord William Bentinck had suffered so severely from the climate, that he had resigned his office. His unpleasant difficulty with the Bishop was now forgotten, and the latter said of him, "I verily believe we shall never see his like again. Had his lordship been educated in Church principles, he would have been nearly perfect."

Lord William's health had been so poor, that he had been unable to attend public worship for some time past, and a special service was held for his benefit, which the Bishop thus describes:

"*Monday, March 10th,* 835.

"Last night I had a most affecting duty. I performed Divine service for the first and last time in Government House. A drawing-room was fitted with a high table, covered with crimson cloth; seats were arranged on each side of the room; all the Court was assembled—aides-de-camp, public and private secretaries, physicians—in number about twenty. My chaplain read the evening prayers (we were both robed), and I preached from the words, 'Come unto Me, all ye that labor and are heavy laden, and I will give you rest.' I used Swartz's sweet notes, as at Tanjore. I spoke and told out 'the whole story,' as Joseph Milner would have expressed it, addressed the conscience, called on the infidel (such were present) to consider his ways, invited the superstitious (such were present) to the simplicity of Christ, and commended the Governor-General and his family and suite to the blessed Jesus during the voyage. They were affected to tears. After the prayer at the conclusion, I pronounced the benediction, and gave it a personal application by going round and laying my hands on the head of each kneeling worshipper, and then returning to my seat and concluding it. The Governor-General and Lady William came up to thank me after service; but they were almost unable to speak for tears. Who can tell what good may be done? I suppose it was the most affecting scene ever witnessed at the departure of a governor-general.

"My own soul is subsiding more and more into God. The excitement of India is gone by; the novelty has ceased; I have run through the first series of duties; human schemes and hopes are exhausted. Now, blessed Jesus! I return to Thee. Do Thou, and Thou only, work in me, and by me, and for me, and through me. Be Thou only glorified. Display Thy grace in the effects of Thy glorious Gospel in the hearts of men."

The day before the Governor-General's departure, the Bishop was requested to administer the Holy Communion at Government House. He makes this record on the 17th of March: "I have performed the solemn service. None were present but Lord and Lady William. After the Communion, they sat down and talked over with me the main things affecting my department. Not a word was said of the sad business of last June. But every thing in matters of detail was conceded to me that I could possibly wish. I then embraced each of them, and bade them farewell."

And now a number of perplexing questions which presented themselves, required all the Bishop's wisdom and prudence and decision of character, rightly to settle. Archdeacon Corrie had gone to England, for consecration as Bishop of Madras; and according to a very absurd custom which had grown up, the senior Presidency chaplain fully expected to be appointed his successor. Bishop Wilson determined that this course should be abandoned, and in the face of the most violent opposition on the part of the aspiring applicant and his friends, he gave the Archdeaconry to Mr. Dealtry, then chaplain of the old church, Calcutta.

The relations between the Bishop of Calcutta and the Church Missionary Society were now definitely settled; Dr. Wilson being unwilling to occupy the position of subserviency to a committee of clergy and laity at home, to which his predecessors had felt obliged to submit. The "Select Vestry" of the cathedral, also, who for years had managed its affairs in their own way, were taught that a Bishop had some rights in his own church, and that he was able to maintain them.

These temporary troubles, however, by no means interrupted Bishop Wilson's ministrations, and he continued to preach with acceptance the Gospel of the grace of God, and to exercise the peculiar functions of his office. On the 13th of October, 1835, we find him once more on shipboard, about to resume his visitation. It was proposed to close the year at Bombay, filling up the brief intervening period by a visit to the Syrian churches, and Goa, on the coast of Malabar. From Bombay, the visitation would extend over the upper provinces, and close at Calcutta, in the spring of 1837.

The little brig which the Government had provided for the Bishop, bore him safely down the Bay of Bengal, around Ceylon and Cape Comorin, and then ascending the coast of Malabar, landed him at Quilon, the entrance-gate to the Syrian churches. The story of these ancient churches is well worth reading, but this is no place to repeat it.

Claiming St. Thomas, the Apostle, as their founder, they have preserved, through long ages, the primitive organization of the Church, and since Dr. Buchanan's visit in 1806, a friendly intercourse has been kept up with them. Bishop Middleton went to see them ten years afterwards, and Bishop Heber corresponded with one of their bishops. We have now to accompany Bishop Wilson, on his visit, in the autumn of 1835.

Landing at Quilon, he preached, confirmed, and ordained, and then set out for the interior, several boats, each rowed by a dozen men, being provided for his party. As they approached Allepie, a station of the Church Missionary Society, the bell was heard sounding sweetly over the waters, and calling to evening service. Though weary with a journey of sixty miles, the Bishop preached to a congregation of about three hundred native Christians, and then at once retired to rest.

The Church missionaries, while laboring amongst the heathen, in the province of

Travancore, were endeavoring, in a prudent way, to correct some of the abuses which had crept into the ancient Syrian Church. It was a delicate task, but they had already accomplished some good, and Bishop Wilson encouraged them to hope for more. With a view of countenancing and aiding this work, he now proceeded to Cottayam, where a college had been established. A grant of land had been made towards its support by the Rajah, and an agreement entered into with the Syrian Metran, or Bishop, that all his candidates for the ministry should enjoy its benefits. The Church Missionary Society had contributed liberally for the establishment of that important institution, on the condition that while the Syrians should have the management of the land, the English missionaries should instruct the students.

This arrangement, while very admirable in theory, was most difficult in practice, and what complicated the whole matter still more, was the character of the Syrian Bishop —who did not enjoy a high reputation for either morality or honesty. It, however, formed no part of Bishop Wilson's plan, to go beyond his own lawful authority, and it was rather as a visitor and an adviser that he had come to Cottyam.

Making his headquarters with the English missionaries, he was waited upon by the Syrian Bishop and a number of the centaurs, or priests, and afterwards inspected their churches, attended their worship, and, by invitation, preached, with his accustomed simplicity and force. A special day was set apart for holding a serious conference with the Syrian Bishop, in regard to the affairs of his Church, a full account of which has been preserved.* The college difficulties, the importance of establishing more schools throughout the country, and the duty of explaining the Gospel to the people—these, and other points, were freely discussed.

On the day following, which was Sunday, Bishop Wilson preached. "I have witnessed," he writes, "the most affecting scene

* Bateman's Life of Bishop Wilson, p. 431, etc.

which I ever could have conceived—two thousand of the ancient Syrian Christians crowding to hear the word of the Gospel in the principal church at Cottayam—the Metropolitan and about forty priests and deacons being present. After their own service, performed in their usual manner, I preached from Rev. iii. 7, 8, for more than an hour, the Rev. Mr. Bayley interpreting. I dwelt on what the Spirit saith unto the Church of Philadelphia: first, as it respects Christ, who addressed the Church; secondly, as it respects the Church itself; thirdly, as to the promise made to it. On this last head I showed them that Christ had set before them an open door by the protection and friendship of the English Church and people. In application, I called on each one present to keep Christ's word, and not deny his name, as to their own salvation.

"Never again shall I behold such a sight. How can I bless God enough for bringing me here at this critical time? for under the present Metran all has been going back."

Chapter Fifteenth.

HASTENING ONWARD TO COCHIN—INTERCOURSE WITH WHITE AND BLACK JEWS—A WORD OF EXHORTATION WHICH WAS NOT VERY FAVORABLY RECEIVED—CONFIRMATION AT COCHIN—VISIT TO SEVERAL SYRIAN CHURCHES—GENERAL IMPRESSIONS CONCERNING THEIR SPIRITUAL STATE—OLD GOA—ST. FRANCIS XAVIER—THE CITY OF CHURCHES—MILITARY STATION AT BELGAUM—SIXTEEN DAYS SPENT IN BOMBAY—PREPARATIONS FOR A LONG LAND JOURNEY.

EARLY on Monday morning, November 23d, Bishop Wilson and his company returned to their boats, and hastened onward to Cochin, where Mr. Risdale, the English missionary, gladly received him. Amongst those who called upon him were deputations from the White and Black Jews, soliciting him to visit their synagogues. He accepted the invitation, and after the usual worship, in the synagogue of the White Jews, he was requested to address some word of exhortation to the people. It was a strange position for a Christian Bishop, but he rose without hesitation, and spoke as follows:

"Children of the God of Abraham, the God of Isaac, and the God of Jacob, hearken:

"We believe, as you do, in the God of Moses, David, Isaiah, and Daniel. The prophet Isaiah says, in one place, 'A virgin shall conceive and bring forth a son,' and in another, 'He shall be despised and rejected of men.' The prophet Zechariah says, 'Thy King cometh unto thee, meek, and having salvation.' The prophet Daniel says, 'After three-score and two weeks, Messiah shall be cut off, but not for himself.' Now, we Christians say that all these things have been exactly fulfilled in our Lord Jesus Christ; that He has come; that He has proved His mission by fulfilling prophecy, by working miracles, by a pure and holy life. Him, through ignorance, your fathers slew and hanged on a tree. You are still expecting a temporal Messiah, with external splendor and glory; we say that the highest glory of our Lord is exhibited in His condescension and humility, in that, though He was rich, yet for our sakes He became poor, and humbled Himself even unto death for us men and for our salvation. We pray you to listen to these things. Seek for the Spirit of God who spake in times past unto the fathers by the prophets. Pray that your hearts may be opened to understand and believe the evidences of the Christian faith, and the Messiahship of the Son of God. There is salvation in none other, for there is none other name given under heaven amongst men whereby we can be saved." * * *

Eyes glanced fiercely and lips curled scornfully as he spoke these words; and whispers were interchanged, as if each one was confirming his neighbor in unbelief. But no outward manifestation of displeasure appeared; and when the discourse was ended, prayer once more arose from the desk, and the "Bishop of Calcutta" (for the words were plainly distinguished) was apparently commended unto God.

The congregation was dismissed, and having examined the parchment rolls of the law, the Bishop visited the synagogue of the Black Jews, and then retired to his quarters at Mr. Risdale's house. On Tuesday, November 14, he confirmed seventy-five young persons in the church at Cochin, and having devoted the next day to a visit to several of the Syrian churches in the northern part of Travancore, he once more returned to the brig and pursued his course. He thus records his impressions concerning this part of his visitation:

"I must pour out my heart, ere the impression is weakened, now that I have completed my visit of ten days to the Syrian churches. And first, I owe humble praises to Almighty God that He has granted me to see the two spots I most eagerly desired, but never thought I should be allowed to visit—the southern scenes of Swartz's labors and the Syrian churches. I have also been permitted to visit them each in the most critical juncture, and have, I trust, been enabled in each to lay the foundation of important service. I was yesterday well enough to write out my sermon on Rev. iii. 7, 8, which Mr. Bayley will immediately translate into Malayalim, and circulate, when printed, amongst the two hundred and fifty clergy, and one hundred thousand laity of the Syrian Church. The Resident will, moreover, immediately meet the senior missionary, and see the Metran, and put things in train to meet my wishes. God only knows what events may happen; but never in my life, I think, was I permitted to render a greater service than in these dear Syrian churches. But, hush, my soul! lest thou rob God of His glory.

"Amongst the general remarks which occur to me whilst reflecting on these churches, one is, that we have here an example of a native ministry in primitive simplicity, living for the most part in their churches, on about eight or ten rupees a month (or ten or twelve pounds a year), their dress white linen, their food rice, eggs, and milk. It was thus Ambrose and Basil and Austin lived, allowing for differences of climate.

"Another remark is, that we have here the primitive use of synods and elections. The Metran himself is chosen by the clergy, two or three being set apart, and then lots drawn. The congregation, also, approves of the priest before he is set over them; and the deacons are nominated in the first instance by lay persons. For all great matters, bishop, priests, and chief laity meet in synods.

"Another primitive custom is, the number of priests and deacons who live at each church. There are generally six or seven; and as, from their poverty, they are frequently unmarried, they live upon the fees. This leads to abuse.

"Another trait is, the high reverence of the people for the sacred office. They distinguish between the bad character of the present Metran and his office. This reverence doubtless partakes of superstition.

"It is a further peculiarity, that each Metran or Metropolitan consecrates his successor early, and then dismisses him to the most distant part of his diocese, to live retired in one of the churches, without allowing him the power of ordination or the privilege of jurisdiction. This is to keep up the apostolical succession.

"Once more. Ecclesiastical and civil suits are brought before the bishop, while criminal cases go before the ruling powers, according to St. Paul's directions to the Corinthians. This is, however, giving way in civil matters, but the ecclesiastical power is complete.

"Again. This is now the only Church, so far as I know, that professes to be governed by the decrees of the Council of Nice, and enforces on her priests, at ordination, obedience to its canons.

"As to the Nestorian and Jacobite errors, they seem to know nothing about them, though the liturgies now in use amongst them employ certainly the Jacobite terms."

The Bishop's next halting-place was Goa—the only remnant of the Portuguese dominions in India, and the head-quarters of Romanism. The Bombay Government had announced his coming, and requested that he might be received with becoming courtesy. This request was more than granted, and every kindness was shown him. Free access was given to the many magnificent churches, and he visited the tomb of St. Francis Xavier on the high festival day set apart to his memory. The following page from the Bishop's journal is worth preserving:

"Old Goa, Convent of the Augustines,
Thursday, December 3d, 1835.

"Here, in the very building where Dr. Buchanan, in 1808, wrote those touching memoranda about Goa, which filled England afterwards with indignation at the Inquisition, I am sitting, with mixed feelings of admiration, grief, and joy. I see some effects of that eminent man's labors. A few years after he wrote, the Inquisition, by the interference of England, was abolished; and in 1830 the entire building was levelled with the ground. I have been walking over the ruins, and it was with difficulty I was pulled up the mounds of overgrown fragments. I looked round on the vast masses with wonder at the mysteries of Providence in the overthrow of this monstrous usurpation. The dungeons were inaccessible, and, indeed, the long, lank, wild herbage springing up all about, rendered the separate divisions of the building indistinct. It seems to have been a quadrangle, with an interior court and cloisters. It adjoined the cathedral and archiepiscopal palace, and is an emblem now, as I hope, of the fall of the kindred establishments of an apostate church in Europe.

"This was, as Dr. Buchanan well expresses it, the City of Churches. In 1590 there were one hundred and fifty thousand Christians in communion with the Church of Rome. Now the number of communicants in the cathedral and different parish churches is about two hundred. As the power of Portugal sank before the Dutch in 1660, and was at length annihilated by the British supremacy, Goa gradually lost its influence. It then became, and was discovered to be, unhealthy. Thus it was deserted, and so remains.

"I have been breakfasting in the cloisters, on provisions brought by Archdeacon Carr, of Bombay, who has joined us, and Captain Le Mesurer, who is appointed to command our escort. On either side I had a monk; one held office in the convent, and spoke a little French. I told him how I admired St. Austin, and had read only a few days since an abridgment of his 'Confessions.' I said, 'We Protestants believe in Jesus Christ as St. Austin did, though you think we are atheists. No; we know we are sinners, and we humbly trust in the merits and death of the Son of God.' 'Je ne suis pas Jésuite, moi; mais je suis Jésus. Non sum Jesuita; sed ego sequor Jesum.' They assented."

On the 5th of December the Bishop left Goa (having returned his best acknowledgments for the kindness which had been extended to him), and paid a hasty visit to the military station at Belgaum, where he preached on the next day to a thousand European troops, and on Monday confirmed and administered the Holy Communion. Five days more brought him to Bombay. Landing early on Sunday morning, he rode at once to St. Thomas' church, and having preached to a large congregation, he was invited to make his home with his old friend, Sir Robert Grant, the Governor. Sixteen days were spent in Bombay, where all things were found at peace. The usual sermons, confirmations, school examinations, and committee meetings took place.

On the 23d of December the Bishop delivered a charge to the clergy, and then began his preparations for a long journey through the upper provinces of India. It was of great importance to reach the Himalaya Mountains, and obtain shelter there before the hot weather set in; and this involved a succession of one hundred marches, and a distance of fifteen hundred miles, through countries in many parts unsettled, and by no means safe. From the commissariat stores of the government, elephants, camels, hackeries or country carts, and tents, with their attendants, were furnished willingly; but each one of the party had to provide for himself servants, bearers, palanquins, horses, and all the many contrivances essential to comfort, and indeed to health, upon a long land journey in India. The camp was gradually formed and sent forward, and soon afterwards the Bishop took leave of his kind friends at Bombay, and set out on his toilsome way.

Chapter Sixteenth.

POONAH AND KIRKEE—NEW YEAR'S BLESSING—READY FOR MARCHING—HORSE AND FOOT—THE SEPOY GUARD—ORDER OF PROCEEDINGS—TEMPERANCE LECTURE—ENTERS THE TERRITORIES OF THE NIZAM—A NICE CHURCH, BUT ONE SELDOM USED—THE EFFECTS OF PLAIN PREACHING, UNDER CERTAIN CIRCUMSTANCES—LAY-READING RECOMMENDED—THE BISHOP OF MADRAS SENDS A WARNING WHICH IS UNHEEDED—BRAVING DANGERS—STANDING UP FOR THE ORDER OF THE CHURCH.

THE last day of the old year and the first day of the new were passed by Bishop Wilson at the great military stations of Poonah and Kirkee.

He thus records his reflections there:

"POONAH, *December* 31, 1835.

"We arrived at this ancient seat of the Mahratta Empire at five o'clock this morning. It is an immense cantonment. It has been fearfully cold. At eight o'clock yesterday morning, the thermometer was 54°. The fine old Mahratta commander of the thirty horsemen who form my escort, **and ride peaceably beside my palanquin, was a celebrated officer under the Peiswah's government, and fought most fiercely against the English only eighteen years since.** The tremendous character of these Mahrattas remains, though they are subdued. My commander came to be introduced to me this morning, bedizened with gold. He had a dark, jutting countenance, eyes fierce and prominent, mustaches black as jet, sword sheathed by his side. This Poonah, with Ahmedabad, was one of the scenes of the acute negociations of the Duke of Wellington in 1803. Even at present, no Mahratta is allowed to go to Bombay without special license.

"*January* 1, 1836.

"A happy, happy new year to my dearest family. A bishop's and a father's blessing rest upon you all. Be encouraged in the good ways of the Lord. Let us grow in grace, and in the knowledge (which includes, in inspired language, faith and love) of our Lord and Saviour Jesus Christ. Let deep, unaffected, heartfelt humility before God, silence, dread of human applause, a willingness to be unknown, a sole reference to the approbation of God the great final Judge, an independence of the frown or flattery of the religious world, be our constant aim. May all this increase in us this new year, immensely difficult as each part of it is."

On new year's day the Bishop preached to five hundred soldiers at Kirkee, and on the day following in the handsome church at Poonah. A Confirmation closed his services at these important stations. By the 4th of January all things were in readiness for the march to Simlah, and the Bishop, accompanied by Archdeacon Carr, his chaplain, captain, and doctor, began his patriarchal life. Two hundred and seventy persons went with him, and formed a motley group of all ranks and callings. First came the soldiers, horse and foot, the former as a guard of honor, but still calculated to render good service; the latter as a defence in a district full of thieves.

The commander of the horsemen has been already described. The men were in strict accord with him—wild and undisciplined Mahrattas, full of fire and pride. They received British pay, but each wore his own dress, provided his own horse, and chose his own weapons. The dress was fanciful, and composed of mingled colors of red, yellow, blue, and white, with a small turban set jauntily upon the head; the horse was active, but full of vice, and incapable of long continued service; the weapons consisted of a long gun, a spear, several swords, and pistols *ad libitum.* These troopers served to carry messages and procure guides.

The Sepoys, on the other hand, guarded the camp at night. Without such precaution in this part of India, few could escape being pillaged. A naked man, with hair shaved close, and skin dark as the night, would glide beneath the cords, cut an opening in the canvass, and strip the tent. All would be conveyed away so silently and imperceptibly, that the inmates, however numerous, would be unconscious of the wrong till the morning light revealed it. Nay, instances were common of the very sheets of the bed being taken from under the sleeper. A tickling feather sufficed, without awaking, to cause a restless movement, and this admitted of a pull. Then came a pause; after which the process is repeated again and again, till the object was attained. And if from any sudden cause the sleeper awakened, and discovering, attempted to seize the thief, a greased body, and a sharp dagger fixed outside the elbow, insured escape. A party who came across the Bishop's route afforded an illustration of all this. They asked to be allowed to pitch their tents close to his guard of soldiers, for the better security. They were willingly allowed to do so, but in the morning there came a message to beg for clothes, since husband, wife, child, and nurse had been robbed of almost all.

But besides the troops thus needed for honor and for safety, each individual of the Bishop's party was provided with a full set of bearers (for no relays were to be met with in these parts) for carrying the palanquin, and running into stations for the Sundays; whilst each hackery, elephant, camel, bullock, and pony had one or more attendants, with wives and families accompanying them. Soon all things fell into order. Each person in the encampment found his proper place, and moved on, day by day, without friction.

Long before dawn the summons to arise and depart was heard; and if the sleeper hesitated, the tapping of his tent-pegs and the collapse of the canvass covering presaged a catastrophe. A cup of coffee was ready at his call; his horse stood at the tent-door; one after another joined the single file, following the troopers and the guide, and keeping close together, lest from the high jungle on either side a tiger should make his spring. Five or six miles were thus slowly passed; and when the sun arose, the Bishop finished the march of ten or twelve miles in his palanquin, and the others on the gallop.

Arrived at the new encampment, a second

set of tents, fac-similes of those just left, stood pitched in the same external order as on the day before; whilst the proper occupant, on entering, found his table, chair, book, writing-case, and pencil arranged precisely as when sleep had closed his eyes on the previous night. All remained the same, but in another scene, and under another sky. Some hours after, the elephants, camels, and carts came up, bringing the tents and baggage. Then daily food was sought, followed by the morning's quiet, the mid-day meal, the evening stroll.

In this style the Bishop made his visitation through this part of India. Divine service and a Confirmation were held at the station called Ahmednuggur, where the breach is still seen which Wellington's great guns made in its strong walls. He also delivered a powerful appeal in behalf of temperance, as the evils of hard-drinking had been seriously felt.

The Bishop now entered the territories of the Nizam, and was escorted to the famous town called Aurungabad, not far off from which was the encampment of English troops. Although the number of Europeans did not exceed thirty, there was a neat church and burial-ground — but, alas! no chaplain, nor any attempt at religious worship. Besides preaching and administering the Lord's Supper, the Bishop baptized a number of native children, whose parents sought this blessing for them.

To show the effect of plain preaching upon the minds of those who had long lived in the neglect of Christian duties, it is said that some were quite alarmed at hearing idolatry denounced, lest the Nizam should be offended at it. The old Colonel commandant had no such fears, but not having attended service before for twenty years, he made up his mind that the sermon was all meant for him, and was so enraged that he would not even say good-bye to the Bishop.

Another officer in authority, but of a different cast of mind, expressed the utmost astonishment. "I came out," he said, "as a boy of fifteen. I have been many years in India, and have been tossed hither and thither. I have been stationed here some years, and have not heard a sermon preached. I never heard such words delivered with such power. I had no idea in my mind of such manly eloquence. I cannot express my feelings."

Before leaving Aurungabad, the Bishop exhorted the residents to assemble every Sunday, and let one of their number read the Church service and a printed sermon, until some better arrangement could be made.

When the Presidency of Bombay was changed for that of Bengal, Archdeacon Carr returned, and another captain took charge of the escort. Here the Bishop received a letter, to which he thus refers:

"The Bishop of Madras has sent me an earnest entreaty to return to Calcutta by sea from Bombay, and not venture the journey to Delhi and the hills. But by this I lose all the advantage of the last three months.

I turn back upon my steps before any adequate cause appears. I leave the Upper Provinces to be visited some other time with increased risk and inconvenience. All here, however, with whom I consult, so fully agree, that I am quite at ease *in foro conscientiæ*, and have resolved to go on, whatever Providence may appoint for me. I am with God."

Braving the dangers of an unsettled country and of deadly disease, the apostolic man pushed onward, only halting for rest, and for the performance of his sacred duties at the stations which he passed. We need not follow him, step by step. Everywhere he endeavored to raise the tone of morality and religion, and to preserve the orderly arrangements of the Church. At a distant station, where he found the chaplain about to read prayers for a Presbyterian minister, who had announced his arrival and expressed a willingness to preach, the Bishop put a stop to the irregular proceedings. It was not, in this case, the result of an advanced liberality, but sprang from ignorance on the part of the chaplain, and an inability to say "No." This was not an isolated instance; and the recurrence of it was checked by a general circular to the clergy.

19*

Chapter Seventeenth.

JYEPOOR—JOURNEY TO DELHI—MOSQUES AND PALACES—HOLY WEEK AT MEERUT—FOUR THOUSAND CHRISTIANS—A WELL-SPENT WEEK—CONFIRMATION—VISITING THE SICK—SUDDEN ILLNESS—HIMALAYA MOUNTAINS—MUSSOORER—BUILDING A CHURCH—DEO GRATIAS—PERILOUS JOURNEY—ARRIVAL AT SIMLAH—FOUR MONTHS' COMPARATIVE REST—PREPARING A VOLUME OF SERMONS FOR THE PRESS.

HAVING performed Divine service and preached several times at Jyepoor, Bishop Wilson reached Delhi on the 26th of March. "After a journey," he writes, "of eighty-nine days, of which fifty-one were, in part, spent at the different stations, and thirty-eight wholly in travelling, I came this morning within sight of the domes and minarets of Delhi. The distant view very much resembled that of Oxford from the Banbury road. A near approach, however, dissipated the delusion, as it displayed the lofty city walls, in excellent repair, stretching as far as the eye could reach. We entered the fortifications at about seven o'clock, after fifteen hours' dâk; and most imposing was the grandeur of the mosques, palaces, and mansions of the ancient monarchy of the world. The red stone of which many of the buildings are constructed is very beautiful. The wide streets, the ample bazaars, the shops, with every kind of elegant wares; the prodigious elephants, used for all purposes; the numerous native carriages, with noble oxen; the children bedizened with finery; the vast elevation of the mosques, fountains, and caravanserais for travellers; the canals full of running water raised in the midst of the streets, all gave me an impression of the magnificence of a city which was once twenty miles square, and counted two millions of inhabitants. May God bless the hundred and thirty Christians, out of the hundred and thirty thousand Hindoos and Mohammedans now constituting the population."

As the Bishop proposed to make a longer

halt at Delhi on his return, he only spent the Sunday before Easter there, at this time, and then pushed on to Meerut, where Holy Week was to be passed. Here, a noble church, capable of holding two thousand persons, had been consecrated by Bishop Heber, in 1824. Several fine regiments of English soldiers, besides a large body of native troops, were stationed at Meerut, the number of Christians in the place being four thousand.

Each day of Holy Week the church was opened for morning prayers, each day the Bishop expounded the Gospel with much tenderness, and each day more than two hundred persons assembled to receive the word at his mouth. On Good Friday and Easter Day the whole body of the military thronged the spacious church. Such a sight called forth all the Bishop's powers. To arrive in time, he had far outstripped the camp, and his sermons were all left behind; but he made fresh ones on each occasion, more suitable, perhaps, because written under present impressions.

Meerut was full of sickness and full of sad hearts, and deep sympathy had been aroused for one of the chaplains into whose house death had again and again entered. As three dear children were in quick succession carried to their burial, the hearts of all were moved, and prepared to receive the word when the Bishop, on Easter Day, addressed his crowded audience from 1 Thess. iv. 13, 14, and spoke of the "child of sorrow consoled by the fact, the benefits, and the prospects of the resurrection." It was hard to decide which was the more affecting sight —that witnessed when hundreds were melted into tears in the great congregation under the power of his appeals, or that when, the public service ended, he went into the house of mourning, and read his sermon once again to the bereaved and weeping mother.

The number presented for Confirmation on Easter Eve had been one hundred and twenty-two; the number of communicants on Easter Day was one hundred and twenty. The evening services, though voluntary as it respected the attendance of the troops, and though the Bishop did not preach, were largely attended; and on Easter Monday and Tuesday the interest continued unabated.

On Wednesday the Bishop preached in a pretty missionary chapel, built by the Begum Sumroo, and under the charge of a catechist named Richards. On this occasion, seventy natives were baptized and confirmed.

On Thursday Divine service was celebrated on occasion of the consecration of a new burial-ground; and on Friday one hundred sick soldiers were visited in hospital, addressed tenderly, and prayed for. The fine schools of the Dragoons and Buffs were also examined.

On Saturday two hours were spent amongst the native Christians, and two hours more in earnest and anxious conference with the chaplains, the mind of one having been long harassed with conscientious scruples on various Church questions.

On Sunday the Bishop preached twice, with his usual energy, but at length he was taken dangerously sick. Fortunately, a skilful physician was at hand, and he soon recovered and pressed onward. On the 16th of April, 1836, he was at the foot of the Himalaya Mountains, the very day arranged for his arrival there, nine months before; so wonderfully had a gracious Providence ordered all his goings.

His first stopping-place, in the ascent, was Mussooree, where was neither chaplain nor church. He preached at Landour, the sanatarium for sick soldiers, and announced to the crowded congregation that he intended to build a church for them, at the same time calling a public meeting to make the necessary arrangements. He thus speaks of the gratifying result:

"MUSSOOREE, *Tuesday, April* 26, 1836, 6.30 A. M.

"Very chilly morning; thermometer 44 degrees; driven in from my walk by the wintry cold. Yesterday also was cold, with a cloudy sky and rain. My poor torrified frame, accustomed for four years to excessive heat, is shrivelled up with this English January weather. But what a blessing such hills are! There were twelve new houses built last season (April to October), and there will be more this. Nor are we without hopes of an English-like country church being built. I was sitting, about eleven o'clock, with two or three gentlemen who had called, amongst whom was Captain Blair, just returned, along the hills from Simlah, when the two leading persons at Meerut, Hamilton and Hutchinson, came to talk with me about the church of which I gave notice on Sunday. We soon warmed. Plans, sites, architects, means of supply were arranged in about two hours. I promised one thousand rupees from the Church-building Fund, two hundred rupees from the Christian Knowledge Society, and two hundred rupees myself. Three gentlemen each subscribed two hundred and one hundred. We ordered our ponies and johnpons (commonly so called, but properly char-palkee—a four-legged chair, carried on two poles by two or more men, and usual on the hills) on the instant, to go and see the three or four places pronounced eligible for sites. The heavens were cloudy, and no sun to dread. We were on the grounds from two to four o'clock, and selected the best spot. Before night Mr. Bateman, my chaplain, had sketched an elevation for a church, fifty feet by twenty-five, to hold two hundred people; and I had finished my letter to Mr. Whiting, the owner of the land. On Monday we hope to be ready for the public meeting. My church-building experience at home comes in, and enables me to speak with decision. *Deo gratias.*

"May 4th. We shall have a church here presently. The beautiful plan was entirely approved by the committee here on Monday, as well as by a scientific officer at Saharunpore, to whom it was submitted. The estimate is three thousand two hundred rupees; and the subscriptions already raised amount to three thousand three hundred rupees. A little hesitation remains about the exact site, because the habitations ramble over a space of four or five miles; but we have two in view, and I hope, before we leave, on May 16th, to lay the first stone.

"May 10 h. God be thanked! I have just returned from measuring out the site for our new church, to be called Christ Church, which Mr. Proby has given us out of his own garden, about one hundred feet by sixty. This will be the first church built in India after the pattern of an English parish church. It will stand on a mountain like Zion, 'beautiful for situation.' The tower is eighteen feet square and thirty-five feet high; the body of the church is fifty-five by twenty-three.

"Monday, May 16th. On Saturday we laid the foundation-stone of Christ Church, Mussooree. The whole Christian population poured out—I suppose four or five hundred persons. The scene on the gently sloping side of the hill was exquisite, and the entire ground around the circuit of the foundations was crowded. The Himalaya Mountains never witnessed such a sight. I began with some prayers from the service for consecrating churches, slightly varied. Then my chaplain read Psalm lxxxvii. Mr. Proby read Haggai 1st, and the whole assembly sang the hundredth psalm. I made a short address. The senior civilian, Mr. Hutchinson, next read the deed of gift. Colonel Young, political agent (the king, in fact, of the Dhoon), read a copy of the inscription. All was now ready, and I descended into the deep cavity in the mountain, and laid the stone in the name of the Father, the Son, and the Holy Ghost. The Lord's Prayer and Benediction closed the service. As we were departing, the band of the Ghoorka regiment struck up the national anthem, which, echoing and re-echoing amongst the mountains, was the finest thing I ever heard. Afterwards I entertained the committee at dinner. We sat down, twenty-one, in camp fashion, each one sending his own chair, knives, forks, plates, and spoons. God be magnified! The whole celebration was unique. It will be the first church raised amidst the eternal snows of Upper India, and all planned, executed, and money raised in a single month. Nine months will finish it."

The journey between Mussooree and Simlah was full of hardships and perils, but it was safely accomplished, and on the 3d of June, at an elevation of seven thousand two hundred feet above the level of the sea, the Bishop makes this record:

"We arrived here this morning, after a march of four hours. Judge of my delight, when a packet of seventy-one letters and papers was placed on my table; and this in addition to forty-three sent out to me on the preceding day. But I am too much fatigued to enter on them. My spirits also are overwhelmed. The impression, on a first reading, is thankfulness to the God and Father of all grace for His goodness to the most unworthy of His creatures.

"Saturday, June 4th. A calm, delightful repose of eight hours, in our nice bungalow; perfect quiet; no jabbering tongues of three or four hundred natives, at half-past two o'clock in the morning; no bugle sounding at four o'clock; no exhausting march of three or four hours. When our camp from below has come up with my books, papers, and implements of business, I hope to sit down for four months' diligent work in this charming climate. But one hundred and fourteen letters rather overwhelm me. I have been at present only able to take them, like Hezekiah, and spread them before the Lord. I have twice done so—expanded them on my desk, turned them over, and prayed for each individual who has written them, especially for the sixty-six brethren assembled in Islington, who signed the letter of January 5th.

"First Sunday after Trinity—June 5th. Blessed be this holy morn! All calm, all inspiring peace and gratitude. I am sitting, at six o'clock in the morning, in my room, with its windows open all around, and the sun just making its way over the eastern hills. There is not a sound to interrupt the moments of communion with the Author and Preserver of my blessings. But something more is wanting than external repose and opportunities—even THY GRACE, *O blessed Saviour!*—or the soul cleaves to the dust still, nor rises ever towards *Thyself.* Quicken *Thou* me according to Thy word! Three of our party are likely to be confined from church from over-fatigue upon the march, and sleeping for nine days in damp tents. They have smart fevers. I owe my own exemption, under God, to the better tents provided for me, and the less fatigue I underwent.

"But I must break off. I have no books, no robes, no sermons, and am waiting for their coming up before the time for service."

The Bishop remained at Simlah four months, the quiet being most grateful to him after a period of constant labor.

There being no clergyman at the station, he celebrated Divine service twice every Sunday, assisted by his chaplain, his leisure hours during the week being occupied in preparing a volume of sermons for the press, to gratify the oft-repeated application of his friends.

Chapter Eighteenth.

AGAIN ON THE MARCH—TRANSITION FROM COOL TO HOT—TAKES BOAT AT ROOPUR—NO VAIN BOAST—THE WATCH-HOUSE OF LAHORE—JOURNEY TO KURNAUL—FIRST ORDINATION OF A BRAHMIN CONVERT—ROMAN CATHOLIC PRIESTS SENT FOR IN HASTE—ARRIVAL AT DELHI—COLONEL SKINNER'S NOBLE VOW—CONSECRATION OF ST. JAMES' CHURCH—IMPRESSIVE SCENE—AGRA — TRYING WHEEL-CARRIAGES — CONDITION OF ROADS—NEW YEAR AT BAREILLY—SOWING IN TEARS, AND REAPING IN JOY — FITTYGHUR — CAWNPORE — DIFFICULTIES SETTLED—EXTENSIVE CHARITIES—FUTTEHPORE — PILGRIM-TAX — ABOLITION OF AN EVIL PRACTICE—DEATH OF BISHOP CORRIE—PASSAGE TO CALCUTTA—THANKSGIVING.

ON the 10th of October, 1836, Bishop Wilson once more began his march. The change from the cool, bracing, mountain air to the sultry climate of the plains was very great, but there was no alternative. Two days' travel brought him to Roopur, on the river Sutlej, where huge boats were in readiness to bear the party onward.

While gliding down the stream, the Bishop was upon the deck, and, looking towards the territory of the Punjab, then scarcely known, exclaimed aloud, "I take possession of this land in the name of my Lord and Master, Jesus Christ." The prosperous condition of missions in that region now, shows that it was no vain boast.

Landing at Lodianal (which was then the watch-house for Lahore, and the frontier station on the English side of the river), he found about one hundred Christians residing there, for whose benefit he at once made arrangements for the erection of a church. The usual services were held, Confirmation and the Holy Communion administered, and a lay-reader appointed.

Passing through Sirhind and Rajpoorah, the Bishop officiated at Umballah, and came next to Kurnaul, an important station, with a large church. Two Sundays were given to this place, a great impression being made by the services. More than a hundred soldiers were confirmed. An ordination was also held—Anund Musseeh, a Brahmin convert of fifteen years' standing, being admitted to deacon's orders. There seemed but one objection to this—the fact that Anund Musseeh's wife remained a heathen, and, by the wise rule of the primitive Church, no candidate could be admitted to the ministry unless his whole family had become Christians. Bishop Wilson hoped for the best. It was the first native he had ordained, and, indeed, the first Brahmin ever admitted to holy orders in the English Church. The new deacon was appointed to labor at Kurnaul, under the direction of the chaplain. Among the multitudes that had attended upon the Bishop's ministrations was a number of Roman Catholics, who afterwards called to thank him for his sermons. Some of the more zealous had become so alarmed, that they sent in haste to Calcutta for a priest, " to stay the plague."

The march was resumed on the 14th of November, and four days afterwards the company reached Delhi. Here the Bishop was to consecrate a church, which had been built at the sole expense of Colonel Skinner —quite a celebrity in his way. Brought up in the camp from his earliest years, he had seen much hard service, and on entering Delhi, with a conquering army, he made a vow, while gazing on its countless domes and minarets, that if he ever possessed the means, he would there erect a temple to the only true God. Twenty years passed by, but he did not forget his vow; and when the government offered to aid him in his work, he nobly insisted on doing it all himself. And now he stood before the Bishop, a tall, stout, dark man of fifty-six, clad in a military dress of blue, silver, and steel, with a heavy helmet on his head, a broadsword at his side, and a red ribbon on his breast—to say that the church was finished, and to beg that it might be consecrated. His sons were Christians, as he was, but his wife remained a Mohammedan, though, as he said with tears, "a better wife, for more than thirty years, no man ever had."

The Bishop instantly drove with him down to the church. It was a beautiful Grecian building, in the form of a cross, with handsome porticoes at each extremity, three of them forming entrances with flights of steps, the fourth closed in and appropriated for the chancel. The body of the building was circular, and surmounted by an ornamented dome, cupola, and cross. The flooring was marble, and a temporary desk and pulpit served for the present occasion. The whole effect was very chaste and beautiful. The Bishop was delighted, and, mindful of the founder, called it St. James, and fixed November 22d for the consecration.

On that day a large congregation assembled, and a very striking and impressive sermon, going a good deal into detail, was preached.

After the consecration, the whole European society of Delhi met at Colonel Skinner's hospitable abode, and expressed their deep gratitude to him. They also requested the publication of the Bishop's sermon as commemorative of the day. A most kindly feeling pervaded every mind.

A Confirmation followed, and the Colonel, with his three sons, knelt at the altar to dedicate himself, as he had previously dedicated his church, to the service of God. The scene was very impressive, and the Bishop's address moved all to tears. At the conclusion, the Colonel himself attempted to express his acknowledgments, but words failed, and he wept silently, whilst the Bishop prayed that the kindness shown to the house of his God might be returned sevenfold into his own bosom.

After a visit of ceremony to the old King of Delhi, and the transaction of much important business, the Bishop proceeded to Agra, where Sir Charles Metcalfe was now the permanent Governor. Three weeks were spent here—a church consecrated, a soldiers' chapel licensed, frequent services held, and much good accomplished.

By this time the Bishop had become very weary of the monotony of camp life, and the disturbed nights in his palanquin, and on leaving Agra he resorted to wheeled carriages and relays of horses, by which he outstripped the slower movements of his large company. The roads were dreadful, and Bishop Heber, who had passed over the same route, compares them to a farm-yard first trodden into deep holes, and then frozen hard; and says, that "though a buggy can go over them, since it can go anywhere, yet they were never meant for buggies nor buggies for them."

Stopping for service at Allyghur, he traversed eighty miles more, and came to Bareilly, where the year 1837 dawned upon him. The attempt to build a church at this place was violently opposed by the officer in command, who insisted that the Government ought to do all this, and he argued the question at his own table, in the presence of his invited guests. The Bishop was taken so completely by surprise, that he burst into tears and attempted no reply. God took care of His own cause, and the party had no sooner left the dining-room than a subscription was opened, and a handsome sum put down. Christ Church, Bareilly, was, in due time, erected.

Another rapid journey of forty-eight miles, through Furreedpore and Futtehgunge to Jellalabad, on January 5th, followed by another of equal distance, varied by a passage across the mighty Ganges on January 6th, brought the Bishop safely to Futtyghur, where he found an excellent chaplain, a good church, and all things in order. Much pleasant intercourse took place here with friends, who were gradually passing down the country from Simlah; the germes of missionary work were watched and encouraged; the church and burial-grounds were consecrated; Divine services were performed; the Holy Sacrament and Confirmation administered; and then the Bishop rejoined the camp for a few days' quiet march. The sportsmen went out and provided the table with wild geese, as on the other side of India it had been furnished with peacocks.

On January 14th the Bishop entered the large station of Cawnpore, and rested in the chaplain's house. He seemed himself to be no worse for the efforts he had made, but all his company suffered greatly, and over some of them the shadow of death for a time had passed. It requires a certain knowledge of India to understand the effect of these forced marches, hurried journeys, and constant exposure.

Cawnpore covered an extent of seven miles, and contained three thousand Christian inhabitants, although it had no church building. The state of society was by no means favorable to true religion, and unpleasant disagreements had taken place between the commanding officer and one of the two resident chaplains. We can not go into details, and can only speak of results. The Bishop went to the bottom of the difficulties and decided the several disturbing questions with his usual promptness. Before his visit was ended, he had preached several times, confirmed, visited schools and hospitals, consecrated four burial-grounds, held an ordination, and laid the corner-stones of two churches—towards the erection of which he gave two thousand rupees out of his own purse. His charities were scattered broadcast over India, and he delighted in nothing more than in helping forward God's great work in that heathen land.

Leaving Cawnpore on the 6th of February, he officiated on Ash-Wednesday at Futtehpoor, and on the 11th inst. was welcomed at Allahabad, by the Rev. Henry Pratt, the chaplain. The grand annual fair was about to close, and immense crowds of pilgrims were paying their tax of one rupee each. The Bishop stood for a long time in the strongly barricaded office, where, by a Christian hand, this tax was taken and a corresponding ticket issued, admitting the bearer to the margin of the sacred stream. Upon the production of the ticket another Christian hand stamped a red signet on the devotee's right arm, which authorized him to bathe, and realize its supposed beatitudes.

The Bishop looked upon the frenzied multitude, the hideous assemblage of idols, the town of straw huts raised on the river banks, the countless flags indicating Brahminical establishments, and the pilgrim, now shaved, bathed, marked, and penniless, retiring from the scene with a little vessel of the sacred water to be carried home—if, indeed, he ever reached his home.

In the contemplation of all this, he says that "he was never so affected since, two years before, he had stood at Juggernaut."

He soon, however, roused himself to effort. He first sought out the despatch of the Home Government in February, 1833, absolutely prohibiting the collection of the tax. He then obtained one of the tickets which was really issued, and is still preserved, numbered 76,902, and bearing a stamp and an inscription in Sanscrit, Persian, and English, for the admission of one Jattree, or pilgrim, to the stream. He gathered up all the statistics also, casting the balance between profits and loss, and inquiring from the best authorities the probable expenditure of human life. And upon all this, as a foundation, he raised the superstructure of a strong personal appeal to the Governor-General.

He wrote, moreover, to the Society for Promoting Christian Knowledge; and his strong statements obtained immediate publicity, and the widest circulation in England and India. Private letters were also written to Fowell Buxton, the Rev. F. Cunningham, and other influential and philanthropic friends; and thus he did his part to overthrow the evil which had been so long and so ably denounced by others. How far his representations may have been effectual in India does not appear. But before the year was ended, the tax was abolished.

The station at Allahabad was very handsome, the situation agreeable, the class of residents superior. A church was rising effectually, though amidst some strife and dissension. A long stay was not required. The usual services were rendered on the one hand and fully appreciated on the other;

and then the Bishop took his passage in the steamer, and dropped down the river on his way to Calcutta. Two days afterwards he heard of the death of Bishop Corrie, of Madras.

"How can I describe my feelings?" he says. "I have this morning heard of the sickness and death of my honored and beloved brother, Bishop Corrie. Oh, what will become of India! Here I am again left alone, with three dioceses on my single hands. Dearest, dear Corrie! Only one year and a quarter in his diocese! It was on the 5th of February that the lamented event took place. Blessed man! he has entered into rest. Never was there a more exalted, meek, consistent Christian. No one—not even Bishop Heber—has filled a more important station in the general propagation of the Gospel in India. All Hindoostan loved him. He inspired universal confidence. There was a gentleness of character, a quietness of spirit, and a boldness in the profession of Christ, which are rarely combined. Well, it is the Lord. His ways are in the deep, and His judgments past finding out. He can raise up instruments at His pleasure. May he be graciously present with his widowed Church."

Mirzapoor and Chunar, the scene of Bishop Corrie's earlier labors, were next visited. Four days were given to the wonders of Benares and the interesting labors of the Church missionaries.

Ghazeepore, Buxar, Dinapore, Monghir, Bhaugulpore, and Rampore Beauleah were successively touched at. "Of all these scenes," the Bishop says, "Heber's description is perfect and most lively. He was then new to them. They met him early. We come to them with minds satiated with sights, and bodies exhausted with heat."

On the 13th of March the Bishop reached home, having spent two years and a half in his visitation. "I cannot enter upon any one duty, this first morning after my arrival in Calcutta," he writes, "without humbly offering my praises to the great Giver of all good for the preservation vouchsafed to His unworthy servant. Thirteen thousand five hundred miles have been traversed, and the whole diocese of India visited, though not in all parts; and now I return in safety and, I can thankfully add, in perfect health. I feel, in truth, far better this morning than when last I left Calcutta. Oh, for internal, spiritual, ecclesiastical, domestic, personal peace in Christ Jesus, amidst the changes and trials which I must, and do, and ought to expect."

Chapter Nineteenth.

HOME WORK ONCE MORE—FUNERAL SERMON FOR BISHOP CORRIE—A FEW WEEKS WELL FILLED UP—SHORT MISSIONARY TOUR—CITY OF KRISHNA—THE FAITHFUL WEITBRECHT — SCRIPTURAL NAMES — AN ELEPHANT TEACHING A LESSON OF PATIENCE—LOSS OF FRIENDS—THE BEGINNING OF 1838—PREDICTION CONCERNING THE "OXFORD SCHOOL" OF THEOLOGY—SERMON BY A BRAHMIN CONVERT—IGNORANCE OF DECORUM—REFLECTIONS ON EASTER DAY—ENTERING UPON HIS SIXTY-FIRST YEAR.

HOME work began once more. The usual Lent services were going on at Calcutta, and Bishop Wilson availed himself of one of these occasions to deliver a funeral sermon for good Bishop Corrie. "All India mourns," was its opening sentence. "We have lost one of the gentlest, meekest, most exalted Christians that our Church has ever known. We have been deprived, for the fifth time, of a chief pastor of our flocks, after a brief, though most honorable and useful Episcopate. We have lost him at the very instant when his presence was required for the solemn office of consecrating a brother Bishop, and thus settling for the first time our Anglican Apostolic Church in India, with her appointed pastors.

An immense congregation filled the cathedral, to show their respect for departed worth.

The Bishop delivered addresses in each of the city churches, confirmed five hundred young persons, and held an ordination, besides attending committee meetings of various Church societies, visiting schools, and performing other work.

The summer proved to be extremely hot, and Calcutta was one huge vapor-bath; but his labors did not stop. In July he made a short missionary tour, to visit a few points which had been passed over before.

Interesting letters describe what was done at two of them.

"Krishnaghur, 130 miles from Calcutta, July 24, 1837.

"We arrived on Saturday at this bigoted

centre of Hindoo idolatry—the city of Krishna. Two pious missionaries of the Church Missionary Society have made a little beginning. I have visited their schools, and examined the children in the Gospels, surrounded by hundreds of heathen spectators, full of curiosity. The children are not Christians; but they replied to my questions with a quickness and decision quite delightful, so that all the crowd heard the word of the Gospel. Besides the schools, the missionaries have small chapels, where they confer daily with the people and preach. Sometimes two or three hundred are collected. The 'lewd people of the baser sort' at times disturb, but none dare injure them. They have no adult converts as yet. We are doing all we can to encourage Christianity and help on this blessed cause."

"BURDWAU, *August 6th*, 1837.

"There is a little church here, very neat and appropriate. Yesterday we spent four or five hours at the mission-house, which is about a mile from the town. I have examined a hundred and fifty native scholars from the villages around. Nothing could be more delightful. Indeed, what I have seen of Mr. and Mrs. Weitbrecht gives me the highest impression of their talents, character, exalted piety, excellent sense, and simplicity of heart. I am charmed and edified.

"There is a little Christian village attached to the premises, of about eighty souls. I visited it. A neat row of cottages, raised a little from the earth, gardens for each family in front (Mr. Weitbrecht is gardener, architect, and every thing), a fine tank before the gardens, three rooms in each cottage, a little nice furniture, beds, tables, chairs, and writing-desk. A picture of Robert Hall adorned one of the walls. The men and women came out as we passed, and I asked, What is this child's name? Theophilus. And this? Abraham. And this? Sarah. What are your several occupations? I am a carpenter. I am a tailor. I am a Hurkaru.

"Thus the cleanliness, comfort, purity, diligence, and honest employments of English villages begin to appear. I do not, of course, speak too confidently; but if life is spared, and, instead of six years, Mr. Weitbrecht continues forty, there is nothing I should not hope. I confirmed nine baptized adults yesterday—all hopeful, and most of them decided Christians.

"Tell my grandchildren that an elephant here had a disease in his eyes. For three days he had been completely blind. His owner, an engineer officer, asked my dear Dr. Webb if he could do anything to relieve the poor animal. The doctor said he would try nitrate of silver, which was a remedy commonly applied to similar diseases in the human eye. The huge animal was ordered to lie down; and at first, on the application of the remedy, raised a most extraordinary roar at the acute pain which it occasioned. The effect, however, was wonderful. The eye was, in a manner, restored, and the animal could partially see. The next day, when he was brought, and heard the doctor's voice, he lay down of himself, placed his enormous head on one side, curled up his trunk, drew in his breath—just like a man about to endure an operation—gave a sigh of relief when it was over, and then, by trunk and gestures, evidently wished to express his gratitude. What sagacity! What a lesson to us of patience!"

Soon after his return from this tour, the Bishop lost two of his friends and associates, Dr. Mill, the Principal of the College, and his private chaplain, Mr. Bateman, both of whom were obliged to go to England for the benefit of their health. A third (Sir Benjamin Malkin), no less dearly loved, was stricken down by death. "I never had such a blow (he writes) in the loss of a friend. Thank God for his religious character; his inward piety (which I doubt not far exceeded what his modest and silent carriage allowed him to speak of); his constant attendance, twice on the Sunday, at church; his delight in religious conversation and family prayer. Yes, I doubt not he is now in the presence of his Redeemer, a **glorified** and happy spirit. But we are indeed left desolate. Calcutta is desolate; his family and circle of friends are desolate; the many religious and benevolent institutions he nourished, are bereaved of one of their purest, ablest, sweetest, and most valuable members. Oh, that I may 'hear the rod, and who hath appointed it!' My daughter gone—my son and chaplain gone—Dr. Mill gone—my most intimate friend now gone! Blessed Jesus! be Thou All to me—daughter, son, chaplain, adviser, friend. Thou all-sufficient Saviour, whose self-existence and infinite fulness for the supply of those that trust in Thee are declared in Thy name—'I AM THAT I AM'—be Thou my refuge."

The beginning of 1838 found the Bishop at home, and rejoicing in some evidences that his efforts for India were beginning to bring forth fruit.

The caste question was quiet, for a time at least, and seventeen missionaries were occupying the field where he had found but two.

About this period, the Bishop examined the writings of Mr. Newman, and others of his school. He writes: "Newman's Prophetical Disquisitions are, as a whole, wrong—grossly, glaringly, dangerously, inconsistently wrong. 'An enemy hath done this,' may be written over the title of his volume. Was ever anything so impudent as the condemnation he passes on Hooker, Jewell, and all the leaders of the Reformation, till he comes down to Laud! 'My soul, come not thou into their secret; unto their assembly, mine honor, be not thou united.' No; if we cannot stand against the reproduction of these school subtleties, we are unworthy of the name of Protestants. If no one brother will unite with me, I am ready to protest alone against this egregious, driveling FATUITY."

A few gleanings from Bishop Wilson's journal will furnish the most interesting account of this period.

"Shalimar. Epiphany, January 6th, 1838. On Thursday evening I had the singular delight of hearing Krishna Mohun Banerjea, my Brahmin convert, preach, for the second time, in English, in the old church. It is an extraordinary thing, surely, that a Hindoo college student, only five or six years ago rescued from the gulf of infidel metaphysical Pantheism, should not only have embraced, but be able to expound and teach, in a very competent manner, the Christian religion. His amazing extent of English knowledge, his good style and propriety of accent, augment the surprise. May God preserve him steady, humble, diligent. I tremble.

"Calcutta, Easter-Eve, April 14th. I have just had three officers of the fleet with me, to beg me to patronize a play to be got up for the famine fund. 'No, gentlemen,' said I, 'that is impossible. You could not wish me to undo all I have been doing my whole life;' and I bowed them out. What a profound ignorance, even of decorum!

"Easter-Day. April 15th. May we rise to greater newness of life with our triumphant Lord! This is my sixth Easter in India. Soon it will be said, 'His bishopric let another take.' Oh, to END WELL! I am jealous over myself. (1) I would examine my heart. (2) I would search into my administration of this vast diocese. (3) I would suspect myself, especially on two points—where the natural selfishness of man blinds his judgment of his own actions—and as to spiritual affections, where decays of grace begin. Lord, raise me up with Christ.

"Calcutta, July 1st. I close to-day the sixtieth, and enter, please God, to-morrow, the sixty-first year of my age. My sermon at the cathedral is from Gen. xxxv. 1, 3. I am, as it were, about to go up with Jacob, and build an altar to the God that appeared to me in the day of my distress, and kept me in the way which I went. How important are the denunciations of Scripture against the world, worldliness, secularity, the name to live when we are dead, leaving our first love, being neither cold nor hot, under the highest professions of knowledge and faith!

These are the dangers I feel, because they creep insensibly on the unconscious heart, and because public life now for forty years has been wearing away the gloss and bloom of internal piety, and rendering the revival of them more difficult. Simplicity once gone, how hard to restore! In this view I look upon the trials sent me as memorials of mercy, warnings, voices, compensating dispensations, needful medicines for the soul, the chastisements of a heavenly Father."

Chapter Twentieth.

ANOTHER CHARGE TO THE CLERGY—"THE TRACTS FOR THE TIMES"—SETTING OUT ON A SECOND VISITATION—REMARKABLE ANSWER TO PRAYER—A NEW FRIEND—GRIEF FOR THE DEATH OF SIR BENJAMIN MALKIN—STATE OF CHURCH AFFAIRS AT MALACCA—GOD'S UNSEARCHABLE JUDGMENTS—SINGAPORE—A WHOLE COMMUNITY "COMING ROUND"—CHITTAGONG—SIR WILLIAM JONES—ARRIVAL OF A NEW CHAPLAIN—THE BISHOP RESUMES HIS OLD COLLEGE DUTIES—COURSE OF LENT LECTURES—PLANS FOR BUILDING A NEW CATHEDRAL—"MY LORD, IT IS ALL YOURS"—LAYING THE CORNER-STONE—THE GREAT WORK BEGUN.

ON the 6th of July, 1838, Bishop Wilson delivered a charge to the assembled clergy in Calcutta. Besides giving a full account of his visitation, and the general condition of missions in India, the charge contained his solemn protest against all doctrines and practices tending to undo the work which cost Cranmer and his fellow-sufferers their lives. The Bishop embarked immediately afterwards, with his good friend Captain Clark, of the brig Hattrass, and set out on his second visitation.

On the 26th of August he thus records God's merciful providence towards them:

"I have been returning grateful thanks to our Redeemer for His answer to our prayers on Friday last. On that morning I commended our ship to the Divine mercy, entreating favorable winds, and begging that the judgment of the captain might be guided what to do; for our stores were falling short, and it seemed almost necessary to return upon our track, the wind was so directly and obstinately adverse. Not an hour had passed afterwards, when the wind changed, we ran by the island of Junk Ceylon, and, instead of putting back, we have been going on steadily for two days. Surely a more remarkable, and, as it were, tangible answer to prayer has seldom occurred to me in the whole course of my life. Accordingly I have composed and delivered a sermon to-day on Ps. cxvi. 1, 2, subject, 'Affectionate gratitude to God the duty of those who have been delivered in answer to prayer.' The divisions were—First: A state of distress supposed. Second: Deliverance in answer to prayer commemorated. Third: Resolutions of grateful love. Application: The *happiness of religion*, which works chiefly by gratitude to God, the fountain of good. The *misery of sin*, which consists of ingratitude and neglect of God, the only source of joy."

Having followed the Bishop so closely in his first visitation, it will be needless for us to do this now. We shall only refer to the most interesting incidents. At Penang, he found in the new Recorder, Sir William Norris, an excellent friend; but the loss of Sir Benjamin Malkin weighed heavily upon his spirits. The Hattrass carried down to the island the first news of his death, and the grief was universal. In the charge recently delivered in Calcutta, the Bishop had publicly borne testimony to his worth; and he attempted to read the extract when addressing the congregation on the first Sunday morning. But the whole audience were in tears, and his own feelings were so overpowered that he was obliged to call the Archdeacon up into the pulpit to finish the quotation.

At Malacca he found the Dutch church, which had been resigned to him, fitted up with all suitable conveniences. A reading-desk was provided, the pulpit was removed, the communion-table inclosed, a vestry built, and new pews erected, so as to increase the accommodation. Porch and belfry were also added, and every thing prepared for him.

Moreover, another of the missionaries connected with the Chinese College and the London Missionary Society, a Mr. Evans, applied to him for admission into holy orders. The decision in his case was postponed, as it had been in the case of Mr. Hughes, till the Society had been communicated with, and had bidden him "God-speed." From that quarter there was no difficulty. But it is sad to record that, when all hinderances were removed, and the way made plain for the reception of these two excellent men, and the fulfilment of their conscientious desires, they both died of cholera within a very short period of each other. The Bishop refers to this melancholy bereavement on January 9th, 1841:

"Conceive my distress at receiving a letter from the Governor of Singapore, dated December 7th, conveying the melancholy account of the death of both Mr. Hughes and Mr. Evans by cholera—the first on November 25th, the second, after interring his friend, on November 28th. No particulars. Each seems to have been seized unexpectedly, and to have died within four hours. Oh, my Saviour! how unsearchable are Thy judgments! Two of the best men in India cut off in the prime of life and health, and just at the moment when plans of usefulness were opening before them. Never since I have been in India has the Church suffered a greater loss. For themselves the change was blessed, but for survivors, alas! the blow is most severe. Still it is the Lord; let Him do what seemeth Him good."

At Singapore, he found the church which had cost him so much care and pains on his former visit, completed and ready for consecration. But it was claimed by a portion of the subscribers, who were not members of the Church of England, as their own property; and a protest against its consecration obtained sixteen signatures, and was presented to him. He never had a harder task than to arrange this matter of common honesty. But he dealt very gently with it. The Governor was firm, and the result good. A public meeting was held to consider the matter, at which the whole case was so clearly explained, that the protest was withdrawn, and the petition for consecration signed by fifty-one persons. All were conciliated. One opponent offered to collect money for an organ; a second undertook to raise a tower; the Archdeacon gave a bell; the Resident, a clock. "I never saw a whole community come round so well," says the Bishop. "To God be the praise!"

Chittagong was now visited. This was a

new station to the Bishop, and the fallow ground had to be broken up. Situated on the coast of Arracan, the novelty of every thing and the exquisite beauty of the scenery charmed him. But there was no church, no Divine service, no Sunday observance, no charitable institutions, no exhibition of Christianity. An occasional visit of the chaplain from Dacca afforded the only means of grace.

Plans were at once set on foot to remedy all this. A public meeting was called, and it was determined to erect a church. Sixteen hundred rupees were contributed on the spot. The Bishop gave five hundred for himself, and five hundred from the Christian Knowledge Society. An application to government and a grant from the Church-building Fund completed the five thousand rupees required; and, as in so many other cases, a church was reared at Chittagong.

A house in the immediate neighborhood, frequented by the celebrated Sir William Jones, was visited with much interest. It stood upon the summit of a hill commanding a magnificent view of the sea on one side, and the mountain range upon the other, and was called Jatlierbad. His study was pointed out; but all was falling into ruins.

The various religious services connected with the visitation were thoroughly appreciated. Not a soul was absent on any occasion. "Never was there a station," says the Bishop, "which needed a visitation more; and never one where we succeeded more completely in the great ends in view. Our host was Mr. H. T. Raikes, son of the excellent chancellor of Chester."

On November 21st he left Chittagong, and on the 23d arrived safely in Calcutta. "I have hardly yet turned round," he says, on entering the palace; "but gratitude for the Divine mercy should swell in my heart, when I consider four months of absence without any one calamity."

In January, 1839, the Bishop was cheered by the arrival of the Rev. John H. Pratt, his new domestic chaplain, the son of his old tutor and dear friend, the Rev. Josiah Pratt.

About this time, two of the Professors of Bishop's College being obliged to leave their posts, on account of failing health, Bishop Wilson came forward, and once more assumed the office of Tutor and Vice-Principal, thus adding greatly to his labors, but recalling, very pleasantly, his earlier days.

A course of Lent Lectures, this season, on "The Lord's Prayer," attracted very large congregations; indeed, the church was so crowded that he began to think the time had come for building a new cathedral. The suggestion was so favorably received, that at the last of the Lent Lectures he announced his intention to the twelve hundred persons present. "I thought," he said, "I should never have such a favorable opportunity again; and that, to express a firm purpose on my part, was one step towards success, amidst the timid, vacillating, shifting population of India."

The Bishop entered upon this work with the utmost enthusiasm, as may be seen from the frequent mention of it in his journal.

Having applied to Colonel Morrison, the Governor of Bengal, to grant him a suitable lot for the cathedral, his request met with the kindest reception. The Bishop makes this note on the 14th of June: "I wrote on the morning of the 12th to the Governor of Bengal, and begged him not to resign me to the Military Board, but to put me at once in possession of my ground, and let me mark it out the same evening. He did so. He wrote a note from Council to Colonel Macleod. At six o'clock in the evening of that day, you would have seen me standing on the ground—about one thousand feet by six hundred—and have heard Colonel Macleod telling me, 'My lord, it is all yours. Choose whatever part you prefer for your cathedral.' I seemed to myself like Moses surveying from Mount Pisgah the promised land. I figured to myself my beautiful spire, rising up two hundred and twenty feet—the fine, deeply-buttressed Gothic nave, chancel, and transepts, marking the massive grandeur of the Christian religion, the magnificent organ, sounding out, 'Thou art the King of glory, O Christ!'—my native presbyters, in their snow-white vestments, walking down the aisles, the Christian neophytes responding in the choir, and *Jesus* acknowledged as the Lord of all.

"But, hush, my foolish heart! All future things are with thy God and Saviour, who oft abashes human projects, and dashes them to pieces like a potter's vessel. God's will be done. I have called the cathedral St. Paul's, to denote the doctrine which will ever be proclaimed by its ministers, and the example of tenderness and fidelity which they will ever exhibit. I have fixed June 18th for issuing my proposals, because it is the anniversary of my leaving England, and completes my seventh year; and because it is the anniversary of the victory of Waterloo, emblematical, I hope, of the spiritual victory of Christ in my cathedral. The next step is to see and get the plans drawn and arranged. I wish I were an architect. But I am not."

The Bishop saved every rupee he could, towards the carrying out of his noble design, and spared no pains to interest his friends, far and near, in the work so dear to his heart. On the 9th of October, the first stone of St. Paul's Cathedral was laid, with solemn ceremonies and an appropriate address. All preliminary measures having been arranged, the work proceeded as rapidly as could be expected.

Chapter Twenty-First.

A MACEDONIAN CRY—WONDERFUL AWAKENING AMONGST THE NATIVES—PUTTING THE SICKLE INTO THE HARVEST—THE BISHOP GOES HIMSELF TO SHARE IN THE GLORIOUS WORK—SEVENTY-TWO NATIVE VILLAGES IN ONE MISSIONARY CIRCUIT—THE BAPTISM AT ANUNDA BASS—"WE RENOUNCE THEM ALL"—THE BISHOP GOES ON HIS WAY REJOICING—A CITY SET ON A HILL—QUIET REBUKE WHICH ACCOMPLISHED ITS PURPOSE—LAND MARCH BEGUN—TWO CHURCHES CONSECRATED AT CAWNPORE—THE SAME DUTY PERFORMED IN OTHER PLACES—"FAINT, YET PURSUING"—A LONG JOURNEY SAFELY ENDED.

ONE day, towards the close of the year 1838, a native, of courteous address and fine bearing, brought the Bishop a message from the missionaries of Krishnaghur, informing him of a general movement amongst the natives towards Christianity. Hundreds were seeking for instruction; many were anxious to be baptized, and there were only two missionaries on the spot, to put the sickle into the ripening harvest.

After a little delay, Archdeacon Dealtry and the Rev. K. M. Banergee were sent down to Krishnaghur, and were met there by two other missionaries. They found the inhabitants of fifty-two villages exceedingly interested in regard to their salvation, and after making all due allowance for worldly and selfish motives which might influence some, there were thousands who seemed to be sincere and earnest.

In February, 1839, the Bishop baptized one hundred and thirty-five native converts at Banipore, and confirmed sixty who had been baptized before his arrival.

Reports coming to him from various quarters concerning the progress of the great work, he soon afterwards left Calcutta, proposing to make an extensive circuit.

He found that the mission in Krishnaghur had already assumed a distinct form. Seventy-two villages were embraced within its circuit, seven hundred converts having been baptized, and several thousand being under a regular course of instruction. The Bishop went from station to station examining, preaching, encouraging, and confirming. He visited Krishnaghur, Solo, Ruttenpoor, Anunda Bass, and Ranobunda; and said he could hardly sleep, from agitation, joy, and anxiety to direct everything aright. He describes the baptism of one hundred and fifty converts at Anunda Bass as follows:

"Never did I feel the beauty of our baptismal and confirmation services so much as this morning—the prayer of thanksgiving of the first, the laying on of hands and supplications of the second. It was the sign and seal and first day, in the eye of others, of the new birth by water and the Spirit. It was the descent of the sanctifying grace of the Holy Ghost.

"We began with examining the candidates for baptism. 'Are you sinners?' 'Yes, we are.' 'How do you hope to obtain forgiveness?' 'By the sacrifice of Christ.' 'What was that sacrifice?' 'We were sinners, and Christ died in our stead.' 'How is your heart to be changed?' 'By the Holy Ghost.'

'Will you renounce all idolatry, feasts, poojahs, and caste?' 'Yes, we renounce them all.' 'Will you renounce the world, the flesh, and the devil?' 'Yes.' 'Will you suffer for Christ's sake?' 'Yes.' 'Will you forgive injuries?' 'Yes.' In a word, I went over all the branches of Christianity with the candidates, and finding from Mr. Deerr that they had for a year or more been under instruction and walking consistently, I begged him to read the baptismal service.

"When we came to the questions, I paused to tell them of the seriousness of the engagement, and I asked the whole congregation of the baptized if they would be witnesses and godparents to these candidates. They shouted out that they would.

"The sight was most touching—one hundred and fifty souls about to enter the Christian Church, and the whole of the Christian village standing sponsors for them! Baptism was then administered; and I stood in the midst, and received them into the ark of Christ's Church. You cannot imagine the intelligent, anxious eyes of the assembly as this was going on."

At Ranobunda, two hundred and fifty were baptized in the same manner; and these additions to the Church raised the whole number to above one thousand.

The foundations of the requisite missionary buildings were next laid, a sub-committee was appointed, the four missionaries now on the field were counselled and encouraged; and then, on November 1st, the Bishop went on his way rejoicing. "A good and great work is evidently going on," he says. "But to oppose this, there is cause to fear—1. Temporal motives. 2. The effect of the relief granted at the time of the inundation. 3. The countenance and presence of so many Padres and Sahibs. 4. The influence of example and popular movement. 5. The instability of the human heart. 6. Satan's infinite craft. *But . . . . Time will show who are tares and who wheat.*"

A certain measure of reaction followed, as it always does; for in the spiritual, as in the natural world, the blossom far exceeds the fruit. It proved so at Krishnaghur. The gathering did not equal the promise; yet a great work had been wrought. A true Church was gathered out of the world of heathenism; and it still stands, like a city set upon a hill.

The Bishop pursued his journey through Berhampore, stopping at Moorshedabad, and then passing on to Beauleach, Patna, Gyah, and Hazeerabagh. At the last-named place he spent Advent Sunday, and administered a quiet rebuke to those who had suffered the church to remain two years in an unfinished condition, by holding Divine service within the four walls, which had neither roof nor floor. The lesson was so salutary, that a pledge was given that the building should be completed in two months.

He preached and performed the usual services at Ghazeepore, Jaunpore, and Benares, and officiated on Christmas at Allahabad, where the river was left and his land march began. Captain Hay, a gentlemanly officer, commanded the camp, which numbered more than two hundred souls—the Bishop travelling sometimes in a little phaeton, and sometimes on his old white "ghoont" or hill-pony.

On the 4th of January, 1840, the company reached Cawnpore, where two churches were consecrated, and thence the Bishop proceeded to Lucknow and Bareilly, where the same agreeable duty was performed.

At Meerut the services were extremely interesting, being attended by a large number of soldiers just returned from the first prosperous campaign in Affghanistan and Caubul. After a short visit to Delhi, the camp moved to Ahmorah, on the mountains, where the corner-stone of another hill-church was laid. The Bishop, although much worn by his travels, continued on his way across the mountains, and on the 24th of April arrived safely at Mussooree, where he remained three weeks. Here, also, a new and beautiful church was consecrated.

From this point he passed on by the lower route through Nahun, to Simlah. His brief sojourn here was characterized by incessant activity. Bidding it adieu, with a devout aspiration for God's blessing upon it, he set out on his return to Calcutta—consecrating churches, and performing other important duties as he went—and reaching home on the 3d of April, 1841. "May God be forever praised and magnified," he says, "for all His goodness and mercy during a year and a half. I have attended church once more, though I took no duty. It will require a few days for my mind to calm down to regular occupations. Oh, for grace, wisdom, power, victory over self, real spirituality, meekness, preparation for suffering!"

Chapter Twenty-Second.

A FEW TROUBLES TO DISTURB THE SMOOTH CURRENT OF EVENTS—OXFORD THEOLOGY AGAIN—THE PLYMOUTH BRETHREN MAKE A CONVERT—EFFORTS TO BRING BACK THE WANDERING SHEEP—WATCHING THE CATHEDRAL—ALL CALCUTTA MAD AFTER THE WORLD—A SHORT VISITATION—SUNDAY AT SYLHET—RIDING IN BOATS AND ON ELEPHANTS—CHIRRA POONJEE—SUPREMACY OF THE HOLY SCRIPTURES DEFENDED—FIRST METROPOLITAN VISITATION—DOINGS AT MADRAS—CASTE DIFFICULTIES—MOVING ONWARD—RHENIA'S TOMB—SYRIAN CHURCHES—DISAPPOINTED HOPES—AT BOMBAY—THANKSGIVING SERMON ON REACHING HOME.

BISHOP WILSON found enough to occupy him, upon his return to Calcutta, and some things which troubled him not a little.

A professor had been sent out from England to fill a vacancy in the college, whose theological opinions were too much in harmony with those of the Newman school to please him, and he endeavored to have him recalled. This request was refused.

Another anxious matter had reference to Mrs. Wilson, who had done a great deal for the promotion of female education in the East. Leaving Calcutta (where she had succeeded admirably), she removed to Augurpara, fourteen miles distant, to take charge of a large orphan asylum. Here she was cut off from the privileges of the Church, and fell in with a denomination called " the Plymouth Brethren," who spared no pains to make a proselyte of her; and, sad to relate, they succeeded in their efforts. The effect of this upon the Bishop's mind we prefer to give in his own words.

"Alas! Mrs. Wilson, of Augurpara, is determined to secede from the Church, and join the Plymouth Brethren. You start! But it is too true. I determined, instantly I heard it, to go down with the Archdeacon and Mr. Pratt, and see what an interview would do, under God's blessing. We conversed with her for two or three hours without the least effect. Yesterday I recapitulated the conversation in an affectionate letter, and offered to pay for the support of a missionary at her station, if the Church Missionary Society would not. All was in vain. We must now endeavor to save the mission and orphans if we can; for this is only the beginning of the fall. My comfort is to cast myself on my Lord Christ, and submit to His righteous will in this sharp affliction. Her apostasy is like a standard-bearer's fainting; and all aggravated by opposite errors. Never was I in such a plunge. Never! But now faith must have her triumph, faith in the power and grace of Christ, faith in His love and wisdom."

The following extract from his private journal will show that his annoyances did not end here:

"April 8th. Every moment is occupied. I have been five days in Calcutta, and four times to my new cathedral. I ride round the scaffolding and framework of the building every morning on my ghoont (as Nehemiah, on his beast, around the desolations of Jerusalem), and watch the progress making, and the different views the cathedral will present. The sun will not allow me to visit it whilst the men are at work.

"Easter-Monday, April 12th. Yesterday we celebrated our Easter. The Governor-General and his family not present; neither were they last Sunday, nor Good Friday. The collection was only one thousand and fifty rupees, instead of five or six thousand, when Lord William and Sir Charles were present. The Governor-General's non-attendance encourages the judges, members of council, commander-in-chief, and higher civilians to absent themselves. We had only about five hundred in church. All Calcutta is mad after the world. French plays are acted at Government House, a new theatre is built, two Sunday papers desecrate the Lord's Day; all is rushing backwards, as to morality and religion, with a refluent tide. I must see what I can do. But the Lord Christ and His Spirit can alone awaken a torpid world like that of India. We must wait and pray."

On the 6th of October, the Bishop left Calcutta, proposing to visit a few stations hitherto omitted, and having spent a short time at Barrackpore, Burdwâu, and Chinsurah, he embarked on a steamer and proceeded to Sylhet and Chirra Poonjee. Writing of Sylhet, he says (under date of Sunday morning, November 7th), "I addressed, pretty strongly, a party of sixteen here, at family prayers, last night, and am now thinking what sermon I can best select for a station where a chaplain has not been for a single day for three years, and where I shall preach only once. I think St. John v. 24, will give me as much scope as any; 'These things I say, that ye might be saved.' May the Lord help me!

"Mr. Sealey's house, in which I am, is perched, like a bird's nest, on the top of a little hill, perhaps one hundred and twenty feet high. But, as it is a cone, the whole circuit of the plains, covered with verdant and thick vegetation, stretches around to the horizon with its green mantle. The contrast with the heats and mosquitoes is inexpressible."

Concerning the other new station, the Bishop thus writes: "Chirra Poonjee. We are four thousand feet above the plains. The thermometer in the garden, at six o'clock in the morning, is 56°; in the house, and with a fire, at eight o'clock, it is 67°. A wild kind of journey of fourteen hours brought us here. We went fifteen miles in a covered boat from Chuttack; then mounted elephants; then I got into a tonjon with bearers; and Mr. Pratt rode on a pony. The place is very bleak; and though doubly and trebly clothed, and sitting by a fire, I am not warm. I have now visited all the hills but Darjeeling.

"Chirra Poonjee is not much frequented, for the water is bad, and the climate a perpetual rain. The distance from Calcutta is only three hundred and sixty miles, but the access is difficult. Sometimes more good is done in these desolate places than in much larger ones.

"At Chuttack (Mr. Inglis') we had a family of seven, and many in tears during the service. Three were confirmed, and the whole seven partook of the Holy Sacrament.

"We are on the south-eastern frontiers of our wonderful empire. The hill people are from Thibet and China. They raise rude altars on the tops of mountains, and offer goats in sacrifice. We had Divine service on Friday; congregation only fifteen, but so attentive, it was delightful to observe them. On Sunday there were two services, and Holy Communion."

On the 24th of August, 1842, the Bishop delivered another charge to his clergy, in which he strongly defended the supremacy of the Holy Scriptures. The same evening he set out on his first metropolitan visitation, proceeding first to Moulmein, Malacca, and Singapore, and then stretching across to Madras, where he landed on the 23d of November.

Before proceeding further, it will be sufficient for us to explain that a Metropolitan is one who presides over the other bishops of a province. It will readily be perceived that this office was one most difficult to be exercised, and which required a large measure of prudence.

Dr. Spencer was the Bishop of Madras—and it was in his diocese that Bishop Wilson began his labors as Metropolitan. Many matters of anxiety had to be discussed, many difficult questions settled, many wounds healed. He stayed twenty days, delivered his charge, preached many times, performed a modified course of duty, and then departed for Ceylon. "Never," he says, "had I a more difficult series of duties to discharge since I came to India. The office of Metropolitan is indeed more important than I could have conceived."

The Bishop of Madras was himself on visitation, and the ship (having landed the Metropolitan at Negapatam, on the coast) carried him on his way to Trincomalee.

From Negapatam, the journey to Tanjore was performed by land; and on December

17th the Bishop of Calcutta found himself once more received into the same Residency (though, alas! death had entered it, and changed the residents), as in former years. To animate these missions, and confirm as Metropolitan the decision he had passed as Bishop, was his great object. He found the mission much strengthened; but caste was not destroyed. Bishop Corrie dealt gently with it; and Bishop Spencer had to learn its evils. The present visit, therefore, was not ill-timed; for seven years had weakened the impression made by the former one in 1836. The venerable Kohlhoff still survived, in his eighty-first year; and the native priest, Nyanapragasen, in his ninety-third.

The native Christians flocked in crowds to church from Tanjore and all the surrounding villages, and were startled by the determined and uncompromising condemnation of caste to which they listened. "On its being honestly and irrevocably abolished," said the Bishop, " the life of these missions depends."

On Christmas Day, services were held for

both Europeans and natives, and four hundred native communicants assembled round the Lord's table. No Confirmation was administered, nor any conference held, because of an unwillingness to interfere in any way with the functions of the diocesan.

A hasty visit was also paid to Trichinopoly; and after five nights' travelling and nine times preaching, in sixteen days, the Bishop returned to Negapatam, and finding his ship ready, sailed for Trincomalee. Here, "being almost worn out," he rested for six days, and was refreshed by the intercourse and friendship of his brother of Madras.

On the 5th of January, 1843, Bishop Wilson embarked at Trincomalee, and, having narrowly escaped shipwreck, arrived safely at Colombo. Here the charge was again delivered, and a clause introduced interdicting the clergy from coffee plantations and speculations. The several stations having been duly visited, the vessel's head was turned towards Tutocorin, whence the southern missions of Tinnevelly, Palamcotta, and

Nazareth (not hitherto visited) were accessible. But wind and weather forbade; and after much difficulty, a landing was effected at a desolate spot called Poovera, about twenty-five miles from Cape Comorin.

No food, no shelter, no means of communication presented themselves for some time. At length a Roman Catholic priest appeared, and a very slender knowledge of Latin enabled him to provide the party with food and bearers. At each halting-place a friend was found in the shape of a missionary of the London Society; and at length, after great fatigue, Palamcotta was reached, in the night of the 29th January, 1843. Seven missionaries were at hand to welcome the Bishop. He at once pronounced the " peace" enjoined by Christ, and then knelt down to return thanks for the preservation and guidance vouchsafed.

Most interesting services commenced the next morning. At dawn of day, one hundred catechists and schoolmasters delivered to him a poetical composition in Tamul, congratulating him on his safe arrival, and on the joy caused by the sight of "his noble face."

Rhenia's tomb was visited, on which appear the words, engraved at his request, "My judgment is with the Lord, and my work with my God." These words, and the tender feelings excited by the visit, were referred to by the Bishop when delivering his charge to twelve missionaries of both the Church societies next day. Station after station was then visited—missionary after missionary conferred with.

"There are glorious beginnings here," he said, "and it is delightful to talk with such calm, well-educated, pious, devoted, sensible men, who know what they are about. I have written to the Bishop of Madras, to express my wonder at these blessed missions, and to say that there must be twenty-four more missionaries sent out—twelve from each society; for now the harvest languishes for want of reapers. What is England about, with her drivelling controversies, whilst India is in vain stretching out her hands to God?"

He went about everywhere preaching—now in finished, now in unfinished churches—now in tents, and now in the open air; but he held that his chief work lay with the missionaries themselves; and when, on the last day of his visit, he found ten surrounding him, he made them a farewell address, condensing the advice he had previously and occasionally given them. In the evening, after Divine service and a sermon by Mr. Pratt, they presented a touching and beautiful address, acknowledging the Bishop's kindness and entreating his prayers.

He turned now to the Syrian churches; and a journey of fourteen hours from Trivandrum brought him first to Quilon, and thence to Cottayam. The reader will not have forgotten what passed at the previous visit. But he has now to learn that all the measures then suggested for the improvement of that ancient Church—for the extension of education, the elevation of the clergy, the eradication of error—had been absolutely rejected. Even the very donation left by the Bishop, which was a kind of first-fruits of an endowment for the Church, was treated as a bribe, and refused. The moment he had retired, the bow returned to its usual bent. The Metran was again in the ascendant, and the Church had sunk too low to desire or to compel a reformation.

So far had this gone, that a covenant was entered into, to forbid all further intercourse with the missionaries, and to withdraw all deacons from the college. What sinister influence might have been at work did not appear. One unworthy clergyman, a chaplain of the company, had travelled through the country, telling the people that crucifixes, and prayers for the dead, and all the superstitions learned from Rome, were right; and that the missionaries and their doctrines were all wrong; but his visit had been short, and he had been forbidden to repeat it.

It needed not this to unveil the matter. Further acquaintance with the Metran and the leading men had developed deep-seated evils, and explained the distaste for any change. And the only course apparently left open was, to set up an open mission. This course had been accordingly adopted by the missionaries, and sanctioned by the Bishop of Madras, under whose license they were now acting.

A great change was thus produced. Handsome churches were in the course of erection. The property attached to the college, which had been jointly held, was now divided. The old buildings had been left for the Syrians, and new ones, already containing seventy pupils, had been raised for the missionaries. Primary schools were multiplying on all hands, and about seven hundred children were under instruction, so that there was good promise for the future. But it was still mingled with regret. It was pleasant to see the light shining in a dark place; but it would have been pleasanter to say of that ancient Church, "Thou hast the dew of thy youth." This regret, however, was unmingled with self-reproach. Our Church had "done what she could." She had held out the right hand of fellowship to the Syrian Church, and been refused; and she could do no more.

At Cottayam, seven missionaries were assembled to receive the Bishop's charge. Divine service was celebrated, the Holy Communion administered, the new college examined, and then he passed on through Allepie to Cochin, and on February 17th embarked for Bombay.

The voyage was long and weary, and he did not arrive till the 13th of March.

"Hurry, pressure, confusion"—such is the first entry in the journal at Bombay. "The Bishop is an 'angel'—so sweet, humble, and spiritually minded;" such is the second entry. The charge was once again delivered; a controversy was settled about the erection of a memorial to the troops who fell in Affghanistan; an address was delivered on laying the foundation-stone of a college in memory of Sir Robert Grant; much pleasant intercourse was held with the governor, Sir George Arthur; all the places endeared by former recollections were revisited; and then, on April 3d, the Bishop once more embarked, and, after calling at Goa on his way, reading through a volume of St. Augustine, and suffering from an attack of gout, he reached Calcutta in safety on Saturday, May 12th.

Thus ended a journey, by land and water, of eight thousand seven hundred miles. On Sunday he preached a thanksgiving sermon from Psalm lxxi. 14, 16, and on Monday he writes:

"I have not yet been able to compose my mind, the change is so great. But, oh! may God give me wisdom and understanding to go in and out before this so great people; and especially to stand firmly and unmoved in defence of the Gospel! I have preached eighty sermons during my absence."

Chapter Twenty-Third.

ON BOARD SHIP—WORKS OF FAITH AND LOVE—SERIOUS ILLNESS—CONSECRATION OF CHURCH AT ALMORAH—PREPARING A BOOK FOR HIS DIOCESE—FAREWELL TO SIMLAH—ANOTHER SEVERE ATTACK—THE BISHOP RETURNS TO CALCUTTA—DEPARTURE FOR ENGLAND—SUMMARY OF THIRTEEN YEARS' LABOR—ONCE MORE AT ISLINGTON—WHAT WAS ACCOMPLISHED DURING HIS VISIT—A LAST FAREWELL—ARRIVAL AT CALCUTTA—"I MUST GO SOFTLY"—CONSECRATION OF THE CATHEDRAL—"DYING CHARGE"—A NEW VISITATION BEGUN.

ON the 17th of October, 1843, Bishop Wilson was again on board a steamer bound for Ghazeepoor. When this point was reached, he left the river and resumed his tent life, journeying through Gornackpoor, Benarch, Allahabad, and Futtehpoor. At the last-named place he closed the year.

Passing onward, through Futtehgur and Bareilly, he came to a new mountain station called Nynee-Thal. The visit to this point was too early in the season, and not a single

European was in residence. Here the Bishop was taken very ill, and was with some difficulty removed to Almorah, where he was confined to the bed for several days. Rallying again, he consecrated a little church, then passed on to Moradabad, Shahjehanpoor, and Meerut; halted for Passion Week and Easter; and then proceeded to Deyrah Dhoon, Landour, and Mussooree. Want of tents for the hill route delayed him till May 14th; and it was not till June 1st that he arrived at Simlah.

"SIMLAH, *June 1st*, 1844.

" Blessed be my God and Saviour for, bringing me once more, after four years, and after a journey of seven months, to this station, and to the same comfortable house which I occupied in 1840. May God assist me during the four or five months of repose. I want to print a volume for my diocese, after eight years—experimental, simple, ecclesiastical, Indian, affectionate, final. It is clearly 'now or never' with a poor, hurried, overwhelmed bishop, like myself. Lord, revive Thy work in the midst of the days. As nature sinks, may grace wax stronger and stronger."

While remaining at Simlah, besides preparing the volume just referred to, he encouraged the erection of a new and larger church, and on the 9th of September laid the corner-stone. On the 17th of October the Bishop left Simlah, to return no more. While tarrying at Umballah, he again became alarmingly ill; and although he hoped the illness would prove to be but a temporary attack, it became indispensable to take a voyage to England. As soon as he was able to move, he turned his face to Calcutta, where he arrived on the 26th of April. Meeting Colonel Forbes at the cathedral, he offered humble thanks, and dedicated the edifice, the architect, and himself to Almighty God. The examination of the candidates and the ordinations followed. Two hundred young persons were confirmed. Affectionate addresses were presented to him, both from the clergy and laity of Calcutta; and he was requested to sit in England for a marble bust, to be placed in the cathedral library.

His fourth visitation was held; a last letter was written to his children, announcing his departure, and laying upon them a solemn charge not to attempt, either by word or deed, to influence his mind, or persuade him to relinquish his conscientious purpose of returning to India; and then, on May 3d, accompanied by his chaplain, he embarked on the Precursor steamer for England, *via* the Red Sea. He had been in India nearly thirteen years, and every power of body and mind had been consecrated to God's service there. Fourteen hundred times had he borne witness publicly to Christ. His substance had been laid upon the altar of sacrifice. He had done much to give the extension of the Episcopate a right bias, and three bishops were now in the field. The control of the Metropolitan was recognized. His relation with the Government was far better understood. Nothing of an ecclesiastical character was done without his cognizance and approval.

Bishop Wilson reached England on the 25th of June. Once more he was in the bosom of his loving family, and in his old home at Islington. Friends flocked to see him from all quarters, and every attention was paid him which the highest respect for his character and services could suggest. Although threatened now and then with a return of his disease—the terrible jungle fever—he was enabled to attend to much important Church business, and occasionally to preach. Queen Victoria presented him with an elegant communion set for his cathedral, and friends sent in their contributions towards the missions in his vast diocese.

But now the time drew nigh when he must bid a last farewell to his dear native land. The romance of India had long since passed away, and he knew all that awaited him there, in the shape of trials, and sacrifices, and labors. But none of these things moved him, and having preached his last sermon at Islington on the 30th of August, 1846, he took an affectionate leave of all who were dearest to him on earth, and with invigorated strength went forth to finish the work which God had given him to do.

Landing at Calcutta, on the 14th of December, he drove to the cathedral, where all the clergy of the city had assembled to welcome his return, and he offered up with them a devout thanksgiving to God.

From this period we must not expect to find the venerable Bishop as active as in earlier years. "I must go softly," he said. "I must take in sail." And so he did. But still the gradual lessening of effort, the contentment with daily duties, and the general superintendence of the Church were varied by many novel incidents and vigorous movements; so that, with chastened expectations, the sunset will be found the pleasantest part of the day.

Eight years had elapsed since the first stone of the new cathedral had been laid, and early in October, 1847, it was ready for consecration. It was designed to answer a threefold purpose. First, it was to be a parish church for a large district of Calcutta; secondly, it was to be served by a body of clergy who, under the designation of a dean and chapter, were to bear a missionary character and to carry out missionary objects; thirdly, it was to be the cathedral of the Metropolitan See of Calcutta—the Bishop's seat being transferred to it, and all episcopal functions performed in it. For the commencement of the second of these designs a large endowment-fund, amounting to nearly £30,000, had been raised, and for the completion of it a similar amount was still required. The annual income thus accruing would have sufficed for the maintenance of six missionary canons, who, with the addition of the archdeacon and six honorary canons, would have constituted the dean and chapter of the cathedral.

But the failure in obtaining the Act of incorporation frustrated this part of the design; and the funds were eventually dis-

Bp. Wilson.　　St. Paul's Cathedral, Calcutta.　　p. 304.

posed of in a way which will be told in its place. For this failure, and the disappointment consequent upon it, the Bishop was in no way responsible. He had done what he could. But the reluctance of the East India Company was not to be overcome. The "better times" for which he waited are yet future.

Of course the consecration of the cathedral was a grand occasion. The Bishop preached for an hour from 2 Chronicles vi. 18. We must allow him to describe the scene. "It was a wonderful sight for India. As I drove to the cathedral at ten o'clock, the whole space around it was filled with carriages of all descriptions, in the most picturesque groupes. The clergy and laity were waiting my arrival, surrounded with multitudes of spectators. I made my way through them with verger and pastoral staff, and then proceeded up the middle alley to the communion-rails. The petition for consecration was then read. I assented; and then the procession began, repeating, as usual, the twenty-fourth Psalm. The other forms having been gone through, the morning service commenced, the organ leading superbly in the chants. Colonel Forbes was sitting near me. I turned to him and said, 'How beautifully the voice is heard!' When I ascended the pulpit, there was all around me a sea of heads, reaching to the doorway and outer steps. At the communion, the thirty-five clergy kneeling at the rails, and the five ministering within, presented to my mind an overwhelming sight. We retired at half-past three o'clock, praising and blessing God for all we had heard and seen. The dinner subsequently went off admirably well. The Governor, members of council, secretaries, clergy, etc., were full of kindness and love. Can I wonder that the Lord sent me a 'thorn in the flesh,' a 'messenger of Satan to buffet me?' No. I rejoice in His chastening hand."

The Bishop, in his journal-letters to his children, relates many things which happened, day by day, but these, though certainly interesting, can hardly be considered of sufficient importance to be permanently preserved in a biography.

In the autumn of 1848, after delivering his "Dying Charge," as he called it, he embarked for Bombay, to enter upon his second visitation as Metropolitan, and his fifth general visitation.

Chapter Twenty-fourth.

RECEPTION AT BOMBAY—COLOMBO—OVERWORK AT MADRAS—ILLNESS—ORDERED TO SEA—NEW PALACE—VISITATION RESUMED—THIRTY-SIX DAYS FULLY OCCUPIED—CONSECRATION OF A CHURCH IN BORNEO—SICKNESS OF PROFESSOR STREET—THE DIFFERENCES BETWEEN GOOD MEN FADING AWAY—GROWING OLD—ANOTHER FAITHFUL CHARGE—PICTURE DRAWN BY THE BISHOP OF VICTORIA—ARRIVAL OF A GRANDSON—INAUGURATION OF THE EAST INDIA RAILWAY—CONSECRATION OF THE BISHOP OF LABUAN.

BISHOP WILSON reached Bombay early in December, 1848, being warmly received by Bishop Carr and his clergy. Here he delivered his charge, and performed various duties belonging to his office as Metropolitan, and then proceeded to Colombo, in Ceylon. On his way thither, he narrowly escaped death, from falling through an open hatchway on the lower deck. At Colombo he was overwhelmed with kindness, and finished the year by preaching in the cathedral before the Governor and a large congregation.

On the first of February we find him at Madras, now left destitute of a bishop, good Dr. Spencer having returned to England with a constitution much shattered by the climate.

Bishop Wilson forgot that he was getting to be an old man, and labored with so little regard to strength, that he was attacked with a low fever, and was hurried off to sea by his physician, although he begged to be permitted to remain long enough to administer Confirmation to several hundred persons who were waiting to receive it. Once more at Calcutta, his recovery was rapid, and he was able to discharge his duties as usual.

Early in September, 1849, he took possession of a new mansion which had been prepared for him, and he thus refers to it in his journal:

"This is the first day I have come over to study, and write, and meditate. I sit in the third story. The prospect is exquisite. The cathedral adjoins the compound; the esplanade stretches unobstructed to the south and south-east; the air is delicious. We shall not come to live here, most likely, till our return from visitation; for we start again, please God, on September 21st. Now I desire to dedicate this new abode to Thy glory, O Lord! May every succeeding bishop live and preach Thy Gospel more and more clearly; may every room have its altar of prayer and praise; and may this change be for the comfort and usefulness of Thy servant's successors, and the glory of Thy great and holy name."

On the 21st of the month his visitation was resumed; and in the usual accommodation boat the Bishop ascended the river to Allahabad, and then dropped down, stopping at the various stations, and performing the required duties. With these stations and duties the reader is now familiar, so that it will be sufficient to state that the journey was performed in safety, and Calcutta regained on January 22d, 1850.

In August of this year he made another circuit, a summary of his labors being thus given by himself: "In thirty-six days I have preached eighteen times. The good seed sown in these visitations is of the last importance. I am satisfied a Bishop does nothing more useful. The tone of religion is raised. Individuals are touched. The clergy are roused. But I shall be glad of rest now, after a journey of two thousand miles, and eight stations, with about a thousand Christians altogether. Most of these have never been visited before. Besides preaching, I have held four confirmations, have consecrated one church and cemetery, and opened two others. Eben-Ezer! Hitherto the Lord hath helped us. Fine weather, a favorable entrance amongst the people, grace sufficient, good health, our beloved Church strengthened, error denounced, Christ alone exalted, many souls, I hope, blessed forever—these have been the characteristics of this visitation."

The Bishop had hardly got rested, after

this journey, before he received a letter from the Bishop of London, begging him to proceed to the island of Borneo, and consecrate the new church recently erected by Sir James Brooke, the Rajah of Sarâwak. A voyage of fourteen weeks and a journey of four thousand miles was thus suggested, by the stroke of a pen, to a Bishop in his seventy-third year! For a moment his heart sank within him; but he had never yet declined the call of duty, and his courage soon revived. He communicated with the Government, and no obstacle presenting itself, he resolved to go.

Setting sail on the 11th of November, and preaching and confirming at various stations by the way, he reached Borneo on the 18th of January, 1851. The church, though not quite covered in, was consecrated amidst an immense assemblage of Chinese, Malays, and Dyaks, from all parts of the island. It was built of iron-wood and the palm-tree, and was a handsome structure.

"Never," said the Bishop, "did I feel such

delight in consecrating a church. The site of it, two years ago, was covered with thick jungle; and Saràwak itself, ten years ago, was desolated by pirates. The whole is next to miraculous; and if the evangelical spirit govern the mission, and strong, heroic men can be sent forth, full of faith and love, glorious things may be anticipated in future years."

Many services were performed by the Bishop on his return to Calcutta, where he landed on the 14th of March.

We referred in a former chapter to the appointment of a professor in the College, with views which gave the Bishop much uneasiness. A few days after his return from Borneo, word was brought that Professor Street was very ill, and desired to see him. He went without delay. "His appearance [says the Bishop] was death-like; and though, from the spasmodic action of the throat, he could not speak, yet his intellect was clear. I simply directed him to the bleeding Lamb, and His one offering for sin, in a few strong words, and then made a short prayer to the same effect, mentioning the righteousness of Christ alone for justification, and the influences of the Holy Spirit for sanctification. I then kissed him, pronounced the benediction, and retired."

As the Bishop was leaving, the dying man raised himself in his bed, and with a great effort said, "God bless your lordship." This was their last interview. The Professor died, and the Bishop officiated at the funeral.

Thus do the differences which divide Churchmen fade away as they approach the borders of that better world where the spirit of controversy and discord can never come.

The Bishop's own health had become so feeble, that when the time for his visitation to the upper provinces returned, he commissioned the Archdeacon to go in his place and look after the affairs of the churches there. Before the Archdeacon's departure, another faithful charge was delivered to the clergy.

In January, 1853, the Bishop of Victoria,

who happened to be in Calcutta at the time, attended his hundred and twenty-second clerical meeting, and thus describes the Bishop of Calcutta as he then appeared:

"It is one of the most noble, as well as one of the most affecting spectacles I have ever witnessed, that of an aged man like him, voluntarily separated in his last years from his beloved family (and my presence when he read his last letters from his children enabled me to perceive how greatly he loved them), and waiting for his summons in humble faith and love. I never before saw him. I should imagine that he is getting feeble in body, but he retains a wonderful amount of mental energy and vigor, and sits up many hours in the day to his desk, reading or writing. The voice fails him most, so that he does not now preach so often, but gives most powerful expositions at morning and evening family devotions."

In the autumn of 1854, the Bishop's eldest grandson, Daniel Frederick Wilson (with his wife), arrived in Calcutta. He was gladly received, admitted into Holy Orders, and, during the short period of his visit, attached to the cathedral.

At the commencement of the year 1854 a short visit was paid to the missionary stations of Krishnaghur and Burdwân; but the more lengthened visitation was reserved for the autumn, when, with Mr. and Mrs. Bloomfield as his companions, the Bishop ascended the river to Allahabad, as in former times.

Here he stayed a week, performing the customary duties, and holding an ordination for three missionary candidates, one of whom was Daoud Singh, of Umritsir, who had maintained a steady Christian character for nine years. Then dropping down the river quietly, he performed, without fatigue, the duties of each successive station, and having " set in order the things that were wanting," he arrived in Calcutta at the close of the year 1854.

A few extracts from the Bishop's journal must suffice for the following year.

"February 5th. On Saturday the East

Indian Railway was publicly inaugurated by the Governor-General. Alcoves with flowers formed a covered way from the Ghât to an ornamented steamer; the other alcoves led up to the station-house. At nine o'clock the Governor-General arrived, and I read a prayer, in my church robes, before the train started. Mr. Fisher, who was acting as archdeacon, and Mr. Bloomfield, in their surplices, read some portions of Holy Scripture. Twenty-four carriages then carried six or seven hundred gentlemen to Burdwin, a distance of sixty-seven miles, in three hours. There a breakfast was prepared, and a number of excellent speeches were afterwards delivered. I reached home by half-past seven, after eleven hours of great heat and fatigue."

Dr. Macdougal, of Borneo, having been appointed Bishop of Labuan, his consecration took place at Calcutta. Bishop Wilson thus refers to it: " Oct. 13.—Things are moving on. The Bishop-elect of Labuan arrived last week; Bishop Smith (Victoria) on the 10th; Bishop and Mrs. Dealtry (Madras) are expected to-morrow. Dr. Macdougal, with his buoyant spirits, fine health, and romantic zeal, is very much liked. All the gentry are asking him to dinner. I have promised him the offertory on Thursday, and a sermon on the 28th, for the benefit of his Sarâwak mission."

"Monday, October 22d. The consecration took place with wonderful success on Thursday. Bishops Dealtry and Smith only just arrived in time. Dealtry preached a glorious sermon, which will be printed. The cathedral was crowded. Hundreds crammed themselves into every corner; but hundreds could get no admission. The sight of the two assistant Bishops conducting the Bishop-elect in his rochet from the distant vestry and presenting him to me was most affecting; and when, having returned to robe himself, he kneeled at the communion rails, the congregation seemed overwhelmed. The presence of three Bishops, in the heart of heathen India, setting apart a Missionary Bishop for the immense field of Borneo, was an event almost miraculous."

Chapter Twenty-Fifth.

LAST CHARGE TO THE CLERGY—SEVENTH VISITATION—BRAVE OLD MAN—FAILING STRENGTH—HIS RESOLUTION TO DIE AT HIS POST—THE INDIAN MUTINY—TRYING THE EFFECTS OF SEA AIR—LAST ORDINATION—CONFINED TO THE BED—"I AM TALKING IN MY SLEEP"—ALL IS PEACE—FUNERAL SOLEMNITIES—BRIEF EPITOME OF HIS LABORS—CHARACTER—HIS BENEFACTIONS—PECULIARITIES.

ON the 23d of October, 1855, Bishop Wilson delivered his last charge to his clergy. It was founded upon the address of St. Paul to the presbyters of the Church at Ephesus, and was full of wholesome and fatherly counsels; and then, though seventy-eight years of age, the brave old man set out on another visitation, his seventh and last. It will be needless to go much into details. The ground passed over was, for the most part, what we are already familiar with. The last Burmese war had, however, greatly enlarged the British possessions in India, and whenever the Bishop visited any new points, he manifested his accustomed energy in having churches established, and other important agencies put in motion. His route included both Madras and Ceylon. He was now subject to more frequent attacks of sickness, and early in the year 1857 he had a fall, which fractured his thigh-bone; but, through the mercy of God, he recovered much more speedily than could have been expected at his advanced age.

His children became more earnest than ever that he should retire from public duty and spend his last days in the bosom of his family. He still insisted, however, that a Bishop should die at his post, and he accordingly remained where he was.

About this time the terrible Indian mutiny began, but this is no place to detail its horrors. While all about him were bewildered and alarmed, the Bishop was calm and collected, and called upon them to look to God for help. Calcutta was crowded with fugitives from the upper provinces, who had barely escaped with their lives, and he cheerfully bore his part towards the relief of their pressing wants.

Towards the last of October his health became so feeble, that he was once more urged to try the effects of a short sea-voyage. On his return to Calcutta he was able to hold an ordination in the cathedral. As the Bishop expressed it, when speaking of his failing health, "The old building may be patched up a little, but it is worn out. The order of nature fixes its speedy dissolution, and the purposes of the 'only wise God' will direct the time and the way."

Again, at the repeated requests of his friends, he went out to the receiving-ship, cruising around the sand-heads, that he might breathe the sea air, but he expected little benefit from the change. His anticipations proved true. He preached to those on board until the 27th of December, when he became so weak that he told those present at Divine service that they would hear his voice no more. He was barely able to reach home. His last days were spent in devotional exercises, deeds of charity, and in setting his house in order, for his departure hence.

As his kind physician sat by his bed-side, on the night of January 1st, 1856, the Bishop said to him, "Now you had better go; I only thought I should like to see you once again before you retired." He was asked to send a summons at any time during the night if he wanted anything, and was then recommended to compose himself to sleep. "SLEEP," he replied, "I AM ASLEEP ALREADY. I AM TALKING IN MY SLEEP." Remarkable words! Death in his case was felt without being realized. It was the "SLEEP OF DEATH."

As the Archdeacon was rising early in the morning to visit the sick-room, a servant came running to call him. Through the night, it appeared, the Bishop had been somewhat restless, as aforetime. At half past five in the morning he had his usual cup of tea; and the bearer, at his wish, combed the few thin, white hairs which were to him "a crown of glory." He then lay down again, and seemed to fall into a doze. His old and faithful Sirdar, the man who had assisted him when fallen in the verandah, the year before, sat with the other servants, just inside the door, waiting and watching.

As time passed on, they were all struck with the unusual stillness. Not a sound was heard—not a movement made. All was silent and motionless. At length they became frightened, and one ran for help. The Archdeacon hurried to the room, and found the Bishop lying calm, and apparently unconscious. Doubtful whether what he saw was life or death, and unwilling to utter a disturbing word, he instantly knelt down and offered up the prayer appointed for a departing soul: "Wash it in the blood of that immaculate Lamb that was slain to take away the sins of the world, that whatever defilements it may have contracted in the midst of this miserable and naughty world, through the lusts of the flesh or the wiles of

Satan, being purged away, it may be presented pure and without spot before Thee." Then, rising from his knees, he kissed the pale, cold cheek, and sought for any lingering signs of life. But none appeared. Without a struggle or a sigh, the soul had left its earthly tenement, and in that hour the MASTER had fulfilled the oft-repeated prayer that his servant might " END WELL."

Soon a little group of mourners stood around the lifeless body. It lay upon a couch in the study where so many hours had been passed, surrounded by books and papers, the eyes closed, the features calm, the hands gently crossed upon the breast. On a table by his side stood the desk so lately opened by his trembling hands. There, also, lay the broken watch, the unfinished letter, and the oft-read Bible. It was a sight inexpressibly affecting to those loving friends, and sent them at once to the throne of grace and the God of all comfort. Thanksgivings mingled with their prayers. They thanked God for having taken to himself the soul of the departed in such perfect peace, and prayed that they might follow him as he had followed Christ. Then, rising from their knees, they went to duty. Bishop Wilson's funeral took place on the 4th of January, and one of the Calcutta journals gives this account of it:

"The mortal remains of this venerable prelate were consigned to their last resting-place at St. Paul's Cathedral, which was in deep mourning, on Monday evening last. At about a quarter after four, P. M., the coffin, which was of mahogany, covered with silk velvet, and suitably adorned, was removed from the Bishop's palace to the cathedral. It was placed on a large bier, borne by twelve English sailors—picked men, of good repute, from H. M. S. Hotspur, then lying in the river—and was followed by the Governor-General, the Lieutenant-Governor, the Members of Council, the Judges of the Supreme Court, the Secretaries, many civil and military officers, almost all the clergy and missionaries, and a large concourse of people of all classes, male and female. In this order the solemn procession arrived at the gate of the cathedral, where it was preceded by the Reverend Messrs. Moule and Burney, the former reading a portion of the burial service, till they entered the church, when the rest of the service was gone through by both of the clergymen above named. The doleful peals of the organ, at the conclusion of the service, added to the solemnity of the occasion; and though the cathedral was crowded to suffocation, the quiet maintained throughout was admirable. Every one vied with his fellow to have a last parting look at the place where the venerable divine's remains were laid, and all seemed impressed with deep sorrow for the loss they had sustained. The coffin is laid immediately under the communion-table, in a vault constructed for the purpose. The bells of all the Established churches sounded their solemn knell from three o'clock to the hour of burial. Thus ended the career of this pious and faithful servant of Christ. Overwhelmed with the care of his flock, he spared neither health nor comfort, at the advanced age of eighty, to watch over their spiritual interests, even to the last moment of his existence. His charitable disposition and kindness of heart will ever be remembered with feelings of deep and lasting gratitude. His end was peace. Well may he have said, with St. Paul, 'I have fought a good fight, I have finished my course, I have kept the faith. Henceforth there is laid up for me a crown of righteousness, which the Lord, the righteous Judge, shall give me in that day.'"

"The Church of England in India," says another newspaper of the day, "when Bishop Wilson arrived, had few chaplains, few churches, imperfect organization, and no influence beyond that which had been gained by Heber, Corrie, Martyn, and a few more, in a comparatively narrow circle. He saw the whole aspect of things changed, and the energy of the Christian community expanding with the increase of the diocese. His preaching in all parts of India, contributions to religious purposes, the example of his zeal, his firmness in resisting doctrinal error, his growing catholicity of spirit, and his private influence concurred powerfully with other causes to strengthen the English Church, to raise the tone of public sentiment, and to attract to India the attention of many who never had thought of her before. We do not propose to sketch minutely his public or his private character, but none who knew Bishop Wilson can have overlooked the steadfastness of his friendships, the warmth of his piety, the clearness of his views, the keenness of his sagacity, the power of his memory, and the undiminished vigor of his understanding to the close.

"His acquaintance with many of the best men of bygone years had given him a fund of interesting knowledge, and his extensive experience of life enabled him to discern the characters of men with remarkably quick penetration. There have been many who have mistaken both his character and manner; many who have been unable to appreciate his sterling excellences and the difficulties of his position; many who have been offended by his preaching. . But his powers were as undoubted as his zeal; and England will cherish his memory. Many such she has given to India for other kinds of public service, and recent intelligence has shown the promptitude of our countrymen to demand for them justice and rewards. But 'peace hath her victories no less renowned than war,' and we doubt not that the finished course of this venerable servant of God will strike a chord in the heart of England, and kindle into life the latent energies of many who will emulate his faith and holiness."

The Bishop left eight thousand volumes for the use of St. Paul's Cathedral; and to his successors in office, his carriages, and many other things which would be useful to them. His legacies to various Church societies and benevolent institutions were large and liberal.

This sketch of Bishop Wilson would hardly be complete without a brief reference to his *peculiarities.* "He suffered them to grow," remarks Mr. Bateman, "and they became marked features. It was not originality or eccentricity so much as peculiarity and oddity—an odd way of saying and doing odd things. And yet there was something of originality in what was thus done and said— something of set purpose—something which gave point to the expression and took firm hold upon the memory. It was discernible in his conversation. To young chaplains, when first they arrived in India, he would say, 'Don't see the sun for two years.' 'Don't eat too much—don't stuff.' 'The most healthy complexion for India is that of a boiled chicken. The great secret of health is a contented mind.'"

Speaking of a missionary who had sought and obtained a chaplaincy, he said, "Ah! he was a true missionary; perhaps there was not a better in India. But Satan and Eve have persuaded him to quit the work."

One of the chaplains in the upper provinces had preached a sermon, in his presence, strongly directed against Calvinism. The argument was elaborate, and claimed to be triumphant. The Bishop said nothing at the time; but when about to step into his palanquin and leave the station, he shook hands kindly with the chaplain's wife, and thanked her for her courtesy, adding, "Please to tell your husband that he has not settled that question."

He would often join together a commendation and a caution. Thus, introducing a chaplain to the Governor, he mentioned him as one "who bids fair to be very valuable to us, if only God keeps him humble."

It appeared in his actions. When ill, once, at Serampore, and unable to join the dinner-circle, a little portion had been sent into his study. He had just eaten it, when the doctor called to inquire after his health. "How are you now, my lord?" "Better, thank you. I have been eating a little dinner." "It will be well for you, then, to lie down by-and-by, and rest for an hour or two." He rang his hand-bell, and when the servants appeared, said, "Lord Sahib sota" (the Lord Bishop sleeps). The next instant he had left the study, lain down in his bed, and covered himself up for sleep, leaving the doctor amazed at the sudden result of his prescription.

It characterized his expositions of Scripture. One of his chaplains was ordered up to the Punjaub, but his wife was unwilling to go. In the course of the morning's reading it happened that this passage occurred: "Having his children and his household in subjection with all gravity." "Now," said the Bishop, commenting on it, "I don't call it having his household in subjection with all gravity, when one of my chaplains is ordered up to Lahore, and his wife says she won't go."

It sometimes appeared in his family devotions. Not that they were too familiar—for familiarity is the mark of a child, and God was indeed his Father and his Friend—but he went very much into detail, and ran sometimes into discussion and narration. He would tell how this thing happened, or that; why he had done this, and why that. If he returned thanks for deliverance from shipwreck, he would tell how the vessel rolled, and the boiler burst, and the passengers were obliged to hold by post and rail.

"I am so surprised at the Bishop's prayers," said a lady who was staying at the palace; "are they really prayers?" "I will tell him what you say," said his chaplain, "and ask him your question." "Tell her," said the Bishop, when this purpose was carried into effect, "to read her Bible, and mark the prayers of Moses, David, Isaiah, Jeremiah, Daniel, Nehemiah, and others; she will find that discussion and narration is the basis of prayer. All these talked with God."

As for his faults, they will have been discerned by the reader long ago. No attempt has been made to disguise or conceal them. They all lay upon the side of hasty impulse, quick action, sharp words, want of consideration for others, a sanguine temperament, something of egotism, and occasional inaccuracy of statement. If the reader has the heart to dwell upon them after the deep self-abasement they have caused and the lowly confessions they have called forth, he is of course at liberty to do so. They are not denied. All with whom the Bishop came in contact have felt them in their turns; but all with one accord enshrined his memory in their hearts; all revere his name; all acknowledge his worth; all assert his piety; all would fain tread in his steps; all say, with Allan Webb, apostrophizing his lifeless body—"A Brave and Noble Soldier; a Wise, Bold Leader. I Esteem it the Greatest Privilege of my Life to have Known and Loved Him."

www.ingramcontent.com/pod-product-compliance
Lightning Source LLC
Chambersburg PA
CBHW031856220426
43663CB00006B/646